FOR THE TEAM

FOR THE TEAM

How to Improve the Youth Sports Experience for Everyone

MEAGAN FRANK

ROWMAN & LITTLEFIELD
Lanham • Boulder • New York • London

Published by Rowman & Littlefield
An imprint of The Rowman & Littlefield Publishing Group, Inc.
4501 Forbes Boulevard, Suite 200, Lanham, Maryland 20706
www.rowman.com
86-90 Paul Street, London EC2A 4NE, United Kingdom

British Library Cataloguing in Publication Information Available

Library of Congress Cataloging-in-Publication Data
Names: Frank, Meagan, 1975– author.
Title: For the team : how to improve the youth sports experience for everyone / Meagan Frank.
Description: Lanham, Maryland : Rowman & Littlefield, [2025] | Includes bibliographical references and index. | Summary: "This book is a unique exploration of the adult's experience as they journey through youth sports. Offering the author's personal discoveries alongside those of coaches, parents, and experts, this book is an invaluable guide for "Team Adult" to learn to effect change and create an emotionally healthy place for kids to learn, play, and grow"— Provided by publisher.
Identifiers: LCCN 2024022358 (print) | LCCN 2024022359 (ebook) | ISBN 9781538198445 (cloth) | ISBN 9781538198452 (epub)
Subjects: LCSH: Sports for children—Social aspects. | Sports for children—Coaching. | Child mental health. Classification: LCC GV709.2 .F63 2025 (print) | LCC GV709.2 (ebook) | DDC 796.083—dc23/eng/20240605
LC record available at https://lccn.loc.gov/2024022358
LC ebook record available at https://lccn.loc.gov/2024022359

CONTENTS

CONTENTS

INTRODUCTION

A Choosing-to-Grow Project: For the Sport of It

ONE DAY IN MARCH, I BEGAN TO WORRY OUR FAMILY WAS IN trouble. From the moment I woke, I felt uncomfortable, agitated, and antsy. It wasn't because we had experienced something terrible or because we were preparing for a difficult day. I was in a funk because we had nothing to do. I hurried past our dry-erase calendar, pissed off about the white space of the day. All four hockey seasons had ended, and the squares on the board wouldn't be filled with new marker colors for another week. I was a mess.

"What are we going to do today?" I asked my husband with an impatient tone. It was an open Saturday, and I should have been enthusiastic and relieved, but instead I sounded dreadful and pained.

"I don't know," he responded indifferently. Things did not get better from there.

The day was contentious. The kids found reasons to spar with one another, I found reasons to be annoyed, my husband found reasons to be irritated, and we never did find anything to do. It was a waste of a day. Losing that time, unnecessarily, bothered me. It felt like detox.

For a millisecond I thought, "Maybe I'm addicted to sports and sports schedules. Am I an enabler? Nah, I can't think that. It would change everything about who I am, who my husband is, and who we imagine our kids could become." I couldn't abandon the thoughts, though. I didn't want to feel so desperately empty at the end of a season.

Fast-forward fifteen years. That dry-erase calendar is now mounted in a new and quieter kitchen with lots of empty Saturdays. In a few months, I'll write the last high school graduation date for our youngest daughter, and then, if I want, I could write "empty nest" in every square. I feel good about it. I really do. I am nostalgic about the ending of this season in my life, but I didn't just coast to get here. If I had, I would feel even more desperately empty than I did all those years ago.

That younger version of me was onto something. Yes, she was sad seasons have to end, and she knew time was literally erasing her days as fast as she was living them, but something bigger was going on, and she couldn't ignore it. She knew she was going to have to grow through where she felt stuck, and she'd need a lot of help to do it.

The pursuit of Choosing to Grow (CTG) has been my life mantra. It began as a desperate prayer when an even younger version of myself almost destroyed our marriage. In no uncertain terms, I became compelled to pursue truth, love, and hope in the name of saving my relationship with my husband. I had studied English in college, so researching and writing my way out of stay-at-home-mom malaise gave me the purpose I needed to save myself and, with the help of my husband, our marriage.

The sports version of CTG was a similar pursuit, but this time I hoped to improve relationships with all the people I love. It is *not* a quick fix, and measuring progress can be frustrating, but the rewards are real, and the benefits reflect investment.

Sports were the reason my husband and I met in college. He wouldn't have been at our two-thousand-student liberal arts school had it not been for Division I hockey, and I chose Colorado College because I could play both Division I soccer and Division III basketball (which I did for one season). Sports defined us, our marriage, and our children, and there was no denying they were a vehicle through which we were raising our kids. I wasn't expecting that my search for wisdom about how to parent athletes would turn out to be a reality check for me. I should have known better, though; it happened the first time I went Choosing to Grow, too.

When I embarked on what I called Choosing to Grow: For the Sport of It in 2011, I didn't think I would actually change the youth sports system, but I sort of hoped I could. I had been watching youth sports change for the worse in a very short amount of time. I wanted to be a better sports parent, a better coach, and a better contributor to the sports landscape—a landscape I had to acknowledge was already ginormous and has grown significantly over the course of my research. According to marketing analysts, as of 2022, the estimated worth of the youth-sports industry in the United States was $39 billion and growing.[1] The global youth-sports industry is projected to be worth $77.6 billion by 2026.[2] In order to understand the little piece of the puzzle that I held as a coach and parent, I had to understand I was working within a much larger puzzle. I know the chance I had to effect big change on the system is probably less than the 2 percent chance our kids had of becoming college athletes, but I did have the capacity to work on the health of our children and our relationships in our family. I tightened the zoom lens dramatically and got to work on myself.

I wanted to learn why I felt the way I felt and behaved the way I did. I wanted open Saturdays to be days filled with laughter and memories instead of bickering and battle. I wanted to learn how to best parent our kids through the storm. By the time I launched the project, our oldest son was eleven, our middle daughter was nine, and our youngest daughter was six. They were all involved in multiple sports, and those sports would definitely influence how they were raised.

Choosing to Grow: For the Sport of It meant I engaged in a number of things. I conducted group conversations or interviews that I called huddles. Groups ranged from three people to a dozen, and nearly sixty people came alongside for that part in 2011–2012. Then I went back seven years later and interviewed thirty of them again to see how the youth sports stories unfolded in their homes. I conducted several one-on-one interviews with experts and youth sports leaders. I distributed a youth sports survey, three separate times, over the span of five years. Approximately five hundred people weighed in with responses to that survey. I assumed various roles, partly out of necessity for the groups with which I was involved, but also partly out of curiosity for this project. In all I did with and for youth sports, I did intentionally and with reflective observation. I coached traveling and recreational soccer teams: boys, girls, and co-ed, ages eight to sixteen in both Minnesota and Wisconsin. I helped create, conduct, and analyze a postseason parent survey for one of the biggest hockey associations in Minnesota. I held board positions for youth soccer and youth hockey organizations totaling six years of commitment. I was a member of the Launch Committee that brought Positive Coaching Alliance to Minnesota (2011–2012). And I read everything I could get my hands on that dealt with emotional intelligence, coaching, parenting, and team building. I also coached a high school boys soccer team for six years and am currently the high school girls coach, which I have been since 2020.

I knew when I took on the Choosing to Grow: For the Sport of It project, it was going to be about much more than the sports information I would gather. My research journey would inform me about how well or how poorly we were parenting our children and coaching the teams we coached. Sports were such an important part of my personal story and my husband's story that, up to that point, it had been the biggest influence on choices we made for our family.

We had moved to the Midwest, twice, for my husband to pursue college hockey coaching. I had accepted an emergency-hire position as a head coach of a college soccer team when our kids were six, four, and ten months old. I continued in that role after moving to Minnesota, even though it meant a fifty-mile one-way commute and I stayed in the "emergency"-hire role for five years. I needed to look at the reasons I did that. We were forced to question everything.

We felt the need to have each of the kids signed up on a sports team every season of the school year. Why? We spent our off-season from the all-encompassing summer work we do running around in pursuit of mite, mini-mite, and miniest-mite hockey careers. Why? More than any of that, though, we couldn't even enjoy a Saturday off. Oh dear God, why?

I knew my husband and I were not in a healthy place with our relationship with sports. Another part of me knew we needed to quickly become healthier because our kids depended on it. Choosing to Grow is a choice to constantly seek wisdom and information so I can determine what parts are within my capacity to affect and what parts I need to let go.

As I looked at some of the darker parts of the youth/high school sports scene, I couldn't help but notice the chaos in human relationships that sometimes exists there. I couldn't help but question the big systemic things that seem unfair and too big to change. All of that was uncovered in my research, and I had to decide why I still felt compelled to live and work there. I had to come to a decision about what I was going to do with what I learned. I decided to accept the parts I can't change, and then I got busy working on the parts that are within my realm of influence.

I've chosen to take the ugly, tattered, uncomfortable parts of my story as an athlete, sports parent, coach, and spouse of a coach and weave them together into something useful. With the very intimate, personal work I've done in my pursuit to heal, I am ready to offer it up to others in hopes it will help build positivity into their lives, too. It is an invitation to those who want to deconstruct and make use of their own experiences. I talk about that through my own lens, of course, but I sought out the accompaniment of experts who helped inspire many of the steps I took to move forward.

Psychologists, sociologists, philosophers, therapists, theologians, and researchers all played a part in what I learned. I found that discipline and control of emotions can change every interaction we have with other people. That truth emerged from every angle I explored.

We, as parents and coaches, inadvertently harm our children as we raise them. Even the very best adults I know admit to their missteps and challenges. Most of us really do have wonderful intentions, but parenting and coaching other human beings is profoundly difficult. We won't always say the right thing, stop ourselves from saying the wrong thing, or perfectly sidle up to an adult in development for whom we care and give them all the nourishment they need for their entire being. Thankfully, there are some best practices I've discovered that armed me to avoid the most-damaging mistakes.

When it comes to how we raise kids in youth and high school sports, there are varying goals. Some folks hope to help their child achieve their athletic potential. Some people want sports to grow character, social skills, and relationships for their kids. Others recognize that achievement in sports could lead to college opportunities or beyond. Those goals were among the goals we had for our kids when we set out on the journey, but even more important to me was enhancing the complete mental, emotional, and physical well-being of our kids, including our relationships with them, as well as their relationships with one another. Due in part to my personal sports story, I set out to guard our family connection with every fiber of my being. I am not alone in my value of quality family time. In a recent poll, the activity listed as the most important activity for Americans is spending time with family.[3] Many of those families enjoy that time together moving in and around sports schedules. So let's invest in making that time fruitful. We do that best when we can get a handle on our emotions.

Emotions are the multicolored mosaic of our lives. We cannot choose their arrival, but the better we can observe them, understand them, and then choose behavior in spite of them, the more capable we are of growing the connection our kids deserve. The members of what I call team adult—the parents, coaches, and administrators in youth and high school sports—will be better able to care for the seeds we have the privilege to plant when we make the choice to grow, too.

A few of the biggest takeaways from my work on the project include the following:

- Adult emotion is the most powerful influence in youth sports. It affects relationships between children and their parents, children and their coaches, and children and their teammates, and it ultimately drives decisions that shape the youth sports landscape. Beyond that, youth sports "businesses" have found a way to capitalize on those emotions.

- Parenting, especially parenting through sport, has evolved for many into a system of directives from adult to child. Children's voices are not solicited when it comes to who they really are, what they really desire, or where they ultimately hope to go in life. That lack of autonomy can be devastating.

- As a collective whole, we have lost sight of playing sport for fun. It is serious business with serious physical, mental, and emotional consequences and especially for those most fully invested in the system. It is also an incredible and increasing financial investment for the vast majority of families who participate.

- For a lot of sporting families, there is a lack of balance with other important human experiences. The all-consuming life of high-level sport starts when kids are entirely too young, and the imbalance is churning out high rates of injury and burnout without a well-rounded balance to healthy living for the athletes and sometimes for entire families.

It has been a wild ride for sure, but I am happy to report that what I discovered about youth sports, high school sports, coaching trends, parent opinions, and processing the emotions surrounding my own personal story has positively changed my life. Our kids are healthfully pursuing active lives, complete with confidence and an understanding of teamwork, work ethic, discipline, and sportsmanship. All the things we wanted them to learn through playing sports have taken root. It was a big decision to get the kids involved in sports, but the bigger and better decision was to choose to grow through their sports journeys with them. Sports are an important way to grow children, and they can become all-encompassing. There is a need for balance, however.

I never made it to an Olympic team, nor did I get paid to play, but like millions of other people around the world, sports have been my life. They are also one of the most influential vehicles of development we, as a society, have chosen to help raise our children. All kids deserve the best and most positive environment to grow there.

My sports story matters, and so does yours. No matter the level you achieved, the accolades you won, or where and how your children or teams are pursuing greatness, your story is unique and important. The energy you expend exploring and understanding your own story will ultimately improve your ability to guide the stories of others.

If you are reading this book, it is because you want to be better. You want to learn through experts and the experiences of others. You are already Choosing to Grow: For the Sport of It, and I want to thank you for that because team adult and the kids we serve are better for it.

As I stand in front of the dry-erase calendar now, I am at peace with white-space Saturdays, I enjoy the comings and goings of seasons I still coach, and I feel proud about what our kids and our family have accomplished through youth sports. Age has a tendency to do that, I guess, but where I've personally arrived hasn't simply happened to me. I've chosen over and over to grow toward this on purpose.

This book is a love letter to the distressed younger version of myself. I want to wrap my arms around her and tell her what she is about to pursue in the name of love and learning will be worth it. She'll enjoy her relationships with her adult children and their father, she'll have a better frame to use for her own sports story, and she'll ultimately arrive at an incredibly healthy emotional space she cannot even imagine quite yet. She'll also have plenty to share with anyone who wants to read about it.

May you, dear readers, find nuggets of wisdom in these pages. May you be inspired to become better versions of yourselves. Let's all go write on our dry-erase calendars that today we have decided to Choose to Grow so we can feel better about whatever it is we need to write on that calendar tomorrow.

Start with Joy

Grow It Early and Guard It Fiercely

SITTING CROSS-LEGGED IN OUR LIVING ROOM WITH OUR FOUR-month-old daughter on my lap, I could hear the patter of little running feet as her two-year-old brother made yet another lap around the first floor. He came toward me from the entryway and stopped in front of me. He threw down his stuffed football, shot his little fists into the air, and then followed his own directions: "Side step . . . side step . . . jiggle, jiggle, jiggle." The room filled with baby and toddler laughter. I couldn't help but laugh, too. He was mimicking a touchdown celebration, and as it is with small children, and especially after we added the jingle, he put the entire experience on a looping replay. I cannot tell you the number of times he performed this fake touchdown run, spike, and dance. It was how I often played with him and his baby sister.

We FaceTimed recently when I thought about this memory. He is now in his twenties and has gotten used to my oft-random conversation starters.

"Hey, I want you to complete my thought," I said.

"Sure. What's up?"

"Side step . . . side step," I said, and then paused.

Grinning, he said, "Jiggle, jiggle, jiggle."

I then asked him about that phrase. He said he knew it was from a Vikings' touchdown celebration, and he remembered participating in the dance quite a bit as a two-year-old. I asked him what emotion the memory evoked for him.

He paused for a second and said, "From my point of view now, this is nostalgic."

I said, "What about when you were a kid? What feeling do you think that touchdown celebration evoked?"

"Elation, I guess," he said, smiling, "or pure joy."

He and I went on to talk about the moments of joy he remembered as a youth playing sports. He admitted that the most joyful experiences he had were outside the constraints of formal competition. He loved fake touchdown celebrations, pond hockey on the lake, and recess soccer games.

"Do you think it's possible to attain joy once formal competition begins?" I asked him.

He thought for a minute and then explained that, as he got older, joy came in winning or from achieving something after long, hard work. I should mention that he experienced winning as a young athlete in a bigger community and many, many losing seasons when he played the less-popular sports in our rural town. For him as a high schooler, joy was achievable when there was a team moment of success: tic-tac-toe passing in hockey or a combination play in soccer that he and his teammates had worked toward and then ultimately achieved. Those were his joy-filled moments.

He was able to identify what Dr. Pamela E. King, a professor of psychology at the Thrive Center for Human Development at Fuller Theological Seminary, says about how we experience joy: "We discover and experience joy in a variety of ways—doing those things we love to do, growing in intimacy or providing for others, and clarifying and coherently pursuing our values. When these domains of the self, others, and values overlap, that is perhaps when we experience the most joy."[1] An individual's contribution to a team achievement after collective effort toward a shared goal definitely creates space for joy.

We play team sports to achieve joy. We watch those sports to feel joy. We wholly recognize that there is necessary and collective sacrifice, pain, and persistence to attain that joy, but it is ultimately joy we pursue. Why else do we subject ourselves to the competition? Sure, there is satisfaction in the pursuit, but if it were just that, then we would all be fine never keeping score. Why else do we put in the sacrifice? For pride? Partially, but pride is more of an individual emotion I cover in the next chapter. Joy is what the entire group can share. There is not an athlete, coach, or parent who wants to invest blood, sweat, tears, and a ridiculous amount of money to only feel the sting of defeat. We do it in hopes we will feel the joy that comes with victory. The key is how we frame victory and how we capture the innocent toddler's joyful touchdown dance and give it room to grow for a child's entire youth sports journey—especially when victory cannot be guaranteed.

The joy of small children is not the same joy tweens or teenagers feel, nor is it the same joy adults have, but the pursuit of joy remains at the root of most athletic endeavors. Joy and elation are what people feel when their team wins, when they contribute positively to a team effort through a great pass, an unlikely basket, a winning goal, or a game-saving goalie stop. Because it seems to be the end goal of this pursuit we call youth sports, it is worth investigating how we grow it in our kids and then guard it once it's there.

To create joy in our children, the adults raising them must attend to their personal joy first. The emotion of small children starts in mirror reflection of the adults around them. They initially are not sure how they should feel about the world, and they look to their caregivers to provide cues. If a baby looks to adults and sees fear in their faces, then they, too, make faces filled with fear. Vanessa LoBue, a professor of psychology at Rutgers University–Newark, writes,

> Newborns develop the ability to discriminate between various emotional expressions pretty early on, including happy, sad, and surprised faces. . . . Between 12 to 18 months of age, babies learn to use information from the mothers' facial expressions as a signal for what to do in new situations. For example, babies avoid playing with a new toy if they see an adult react fearfully toward it.[2]

If a parent is sad, then the children around them absorb it. Similarly, if parents are joyful, then most often their children are, too.

Luckily, sport offers the perfect environment to create joy for both kids and adults. They are built on games and play, after all. The challenge is to maintain the integrity of what games are meant to provide: fun and enjoyment. Child's play is enough to create introductory joy around sport for kids. It's important to encourage and welcome the joyful movements of children as they acquire them, perfect them, and then purposefully use them for their own joy-filled moments of achievement.

Young children love to play. At first the play happens individually. The smallest of children barely know their own body in the spaces they occupy, and the toys and games in front of them inspire joyful curiosity that we hear in their laughter. Physical exploration and celebrating the varied uses of their bodies can and should be a most joyous experience. Have you ever watched a baby discover that the floating hand attached to their arm is their own? There are some really cute videos on YouTube that capture this magical moment. Very often the reaction of the baby is awe and grand curiosity. Wouldn't it be something if we could capture that joyful discovery and experience it with every physical development? Here are a few suggestions for harnessing the power of joy at the various stages of childhood and adolescence (see figure 1.1).

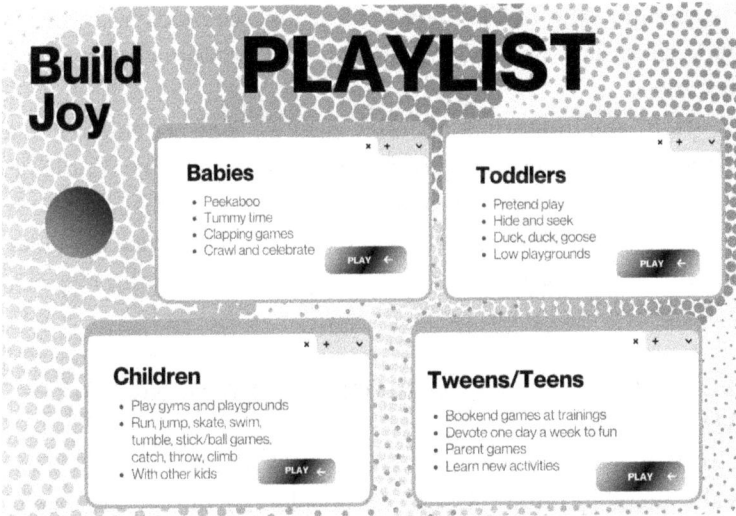

Build Joy **PLAYLIST**

Babies
- Peekaboo
- Tummy time
- Clapping games
- Crawl and celebrate

PLAY ←

Toddlers
- Pretend play
- Hide and seek
- Duck, duck, goose
- Low playgrounds

PLAY ←

Children
- Play gyms and playgrounds
- Run, jump, skate, swim, tumble, stick/ball games, catch, throw, climb
- With other kids

PLAY ←

Tweens/Teens
- Bookend games at trainings
- Devote one day a week to fun
- Parent games
- Learn new activities

PLAY ←

Figure 1.1. Movement Playlist Suggestions for All Ages

BABIES: ENGAGE, COMMUNICATE, AND PLAY

From the moment each of our children arrived, I was so curious about them. I wanted to know them completely and provide the most enriching environment I could. I'm pretty keen on communication, so some of the first physical movements I chose to teach our kids was baby sign language. Beginning when they were about six or seven months, I used hand signs at the same time as I spoke words like *more, milk, water, cheese, apple, banana, eat, all done, medicine, bathroom, please, thank you,* and *sorry.* Those signs started coming back from the babies beginning when they were each nine or ten months old. They became regularly proficient by twelve to thirteen months. Psychologist Dr. Gwyneth Doherty-Sneddon of the University of Stirling in the United Kingdom reviewed research about the efficacy of baby signing, and she found, "Communication is at the heart of child development, be it cognitive, social, emotional or behavioral."[3] What the experts had predicted, and I had hoped for, certainly happened in our house. We had fewer temper tantrums, and it was a fun family-bonding exercise.

Baby signing provided communication, connection, practice with controlled physical movement, and occasional party-trick attention.

It is also important to offer play as soon as children are moving. According to an article from Johns Hopkins Medicine, "Studies have shown that parents who play with their baby can help promote their cognitive development, and as they get older, the children will do better with language and math skills. Play also helps promote physical development."[4]

TODDLERS AND YOUNG CHILDREN: GET MOVING AND MAKE IT FUN

Can you speak movement? Would you consider yourself physically literate? Physically literate people can run; throw; catch; skate; jump; swim; hit something with a stick, both in the air and on the ground; kick a ball; and tumble. If you are an athlete, then you are among the physically literate. You speak movement. We all have the capacity to learn athletic movements, and like a language, the window for that type of learning is when children are young.

While recruiting for college soccer players, I could tell which kids had been exposed to more movements than are required to play soccer. I could see the comfort of gymnasts when their bodies were airborne. They knew how to fall well or roll out of a situation. Hockey players had really good core control, and their balance and strength were evident. Basketball players had agile footwork and an ease in their defensive posture. Cross-country and track runners had the stride and stamina of, well, runners. If you study the movements of athletes as they move for their sports, you might notice the ways they trained their childhood muscles.

When and how they learn to move determines everything. Comfort and confidence in physical movement are the building blocks to joyful participation. There are a number of programs to capitalize on the windows of learning physical movement. One such program is the comprehensive and continually evolving Sport for Life program out of Canada. They've done the legwork, so there is no need to reinvent the wheel here, but essentially it suggests exposing children to appropriate and technically sound movement in a variety of activities starting when they are babies. Their website (https://activeforlife.com) is chock-full of research, resources, information, and suggestions for people of all walks of life to turn child's play into physical literacy. This approach enhances the goal of people who want to help their developing children push toward their personal athletic potential. It is also a program geared to keep people moving throughout their lives.[5] Joy seeds are planted here.

In a nutshell, growing athletes begins with growing joy. Encourage them by playing with them as babies, and then as they get older, play with them in a physical way every day: in the backyard, at the park, with soft things in the family room. Play and joy go hand in hand, and joy begets effort and motivation.

Play games with them like duck, duck, goose; hide and seek; and tag. Then expose them to as many movements as you can. When they become proficient, introduce running, hanging on a bar, monkey-bar traversing, tumbling, jumping, and swimming. The progression is to then add other elements, like balls to kick or throw. Let them play with tennis balls, small footballs, or pool noodles as javelins or bats. They eventually will be able to catch thrown objects and swing at them in midair. Throwing or shooting a ball into a hoop or basket would be next, along with ice skating, skateboarding, and skiing. None of this has to necessarily be formal in nature. Even if you yourself do not know how to do these movements well, learning alongside your children is part of how joy grows for them. Kids experience so much joy when they have a chance to play *with* their parents and not just *for* them. If you do not believe me, ask the parents attending a youth practice to join the kids for a giant game of blob tag or take part in a parent-kid game. It will be one of the more joy-filled memories of the season.

All children have a right to the sort of happiness that movement can invoke, no matter their physical or intellectual abilities. I've been a part of several joyful experiences watching every type of athlete compete. I've cheered for Special Olympics hockey and bocce players, scored games for a Special Olympics basketball tournament, and volunteered several years running the sideline for power soccer games played with wheelchairs. Joy is palpable for all kids who get the chance to play, no matter how they manage to do it.

I'm not the only one who believes that. The eighth right listed on Project Play's Children's Rights in Sports is "To enjoy themselves. Children have the right to participate in activities they consider fun, and which foster the development of friendships and social bonds."[6] Small children need to play partly for the physical joy but eventually also for the social connectivity available. Both are so paramount to their healthy development. By the time they enter tween and teenage years, they are more physically competent, and the demands of performance and achievement become more intense, but I contend there needs to be an effort to let joy seeds grow for them, too.

TWEENS AND TEENS: KEEP THE FUN, ENCOURAGE THE JOY

We've raised three children through the tween and teenage years, and I have been coaching teenagers for more than a decade. As dramatic as the sullen teen character is in their portrayal in movies and shows, I can attest that a sadder version of kids certainly shows up more regularly starting toward the end of middle school and through much of high school. The hooded, moody version tends to find happier moments with their peers. Friends become increasingly influential for teenage athletes. It looks a little different with each athlete, but adult energy, especially as it relates to physical competition, puts a lot of pressure on teenage athletes, and probably not intentionally, the joy element of the games is not as highly valued. It matters that athletes are then surrounded by the right sort of positive teammates and peers because they will certainly influence their experience. In an article titled "Understanding Enjoyment in Youth Sport: A Developmental Perspective," researchers Paul McCarthy, Marc Jones, and David Clark-Carter argue, "Positive interactions with peers and significant adults strongly influence the enjoyment experienced in youth sports in particular."[7] If we as team adult want to affect the level of enjoyment kids have while they participate in sports, then we need to be mindful of their joy quotient and surround them with joyful people.

Professional soccer player John Wilson talked about his journey through joy in a TED Talk in 2014. He talked about when he had joy, how he lost it, and his decision to reclaim it. He had a coach who encouraged him as a young player to "listen with your eyes and your ears" and a mother who always encouraged him to have fun—directives that would certainly grow joy. As he moved through the ranks, however, he began listening more to the directives to score and win, and the mantra he internalized, "You gotta make it," replaced his fun energy. It started to be that his "joy for the game was directly linked to the result of the game." He was only happy if they won or if he scored. Wilson said, "If you play for the joy of sport, successful development as a person *and* as a player is possible."[8] Too many athletes evolve into the joyless version that Wilson became.

So how do we guard joy that is built in small children? One way it is grown and guarded is to create success. Remember, joy *does* exist with success and winning. Parents know this, thus the pick-up-and-move-from-an-unsuccessful-situation-to-the-team-that-will-provide-the-most-successful-opportunities attitude. That works for a few people. Winning all the time is not an attainable source of joy for everyone, however, and especially those who do not have the resources to pursue the highest level of achievement in their respective sports. Luckily, it is possible to create a joy-filled environment for all athletes, no matter their potential for winning. Success can be measured in a number of ways.

Amanda Visek from the Milken Institute School of Public Health at George Washington University has been studying youth sports and specifically fun in youth sports for several years: "Her federally funded, applied research includes the FUN MAPS, the latest sport science advancement [that] are the scientific blueprints for the fun integration theory, the first-ever fully conceptual framework for optimizing youth's positive sports experiences, both in their childhood and through their adolescence."[9] Tapping into joy and fun can happen in any youth sports environment, but it takes even more intentionality as the kids get older.

Visek has identified eleven fun determinants that comprise the comprehensive FUN MAPS. Thankfully, many of them are something upon which team adult can focus and implement alongside kids on their journey. Positive coaching, team rituals, swag, game-time support, learning and improving, games, team friendships, practice, trying hard, mental bonuses, and being a good sport are the determinants for fun that interviewed athletes shared.[10] This list is not exclusive to young children, and I can attest to the fact that these determinants exist at the high school level, as well. Creating a positive, fun, and joy-filled environment takes time, but it is possible. Some of the things I have adopted to inject joy into the soccer teams I've coached have included:

- Beginning and ending my practices with a game. I stopped ending with conditioning a long time ago. Conditioning is either worked into the drills, or if we really need to spend time on it, then I'll put it smack dab in the middle of our trainings. I want the kids to do something joyful when they arrive and just before they leave the field.

- Friday fun days each week. The players determine the theme, which includes fun socks, crazy hair, or maybe playing something other than soccer. Fun is the focus for that day.
- Breakfast book club monthly meetings. We eat food, chat about gratitude, grow relationships, and dig into the things that matter. I know, at least for me, they are joyful, and I think they are for the kids, too.
- Monthly socials outside school doing something joyful.

My goals as a coach are twofold: (1) train and prepare the athletes to compete and (2) create an environment of connection and enjoyment in every way possible. I hope they create wonderful relationships with their teammates and they want to be active for their entire lives. Of those hundreds of people I surveyed, approximately 70 percent believe one of the goals of youth sports should be to create people who are active for life. It matters how people feel about a lifelong commitment to something, and it is hard to stick with those things we do not enjoy. A lifelong love of being active depends on the presence of joy.

Joy is connected to motivation and effective for commitment. As the adults in the room, we need to be aware of the fuel used to motivate athletes. Is it toxic positivity or joy? An interesting distinction is laid out by Positive Performance (a mindset coach academy). Toxic positivity "tells us to quickly move past negative emotions by slapping a motivational phrase on the problem or dismissing the pain of it altogether," while joy "carves out room to feel all of it; the disappointment, regret, embarrassment. To look it square in the face and, in spite of those feelings (maybe even BECAUSE of those feelings) choose it over and over again. . . . You can find JOY in that."[11] Because we want authentic joy and not toxic positivity, we need to look at and work through those negative and harder emotions, too—emotions like shame and pride.

Choose Love

Above Shameful Pride

IN MY SECOND OR THIRD YEAR AS A COLLEGE COACH, A PLAYER named Nicole was cut from the team. She nodded her head in agreement as I shared with her my assessment of her as an athlete, and then she asked if she would be able to continue with the program as a manager. She was such a positive person, and the players adored her. I was thrilled about her request. At a game on the other side of the state, as the team was warming up, a group of people arrived at the stadium. They were carrying signs to cheer on the team and several that named Nicole specifically because they were there to cheer for her. She was not going to be in uniform, she was not going to step on the field, but her family and friends brought with them a little cheering section and a ton of unconditional love. It did not take long to connect the loving support of her family with her admirable character.

You want children in your care to be good people? Love them. You want them to find success? Love them. You want them to be healthy and to achieve their greatest potential for wealth? Love them. Abraham Maslow places love smack dab in the middle of his pyramid of hierarchical human needs, and Harvard's study of adult development found loved children do much better through life.[1] Love is the key.[2] George Vaillant, professor of psychiatry at

Harvard Medical School, wrote in an article about the Harvard study, "Achievement of high military rank in World War II correlated more highly with a warm childhood than with social class, athletic success or intelligence. . . . Children who fail to learn basic love and trust at home are handicapped later in mastering the assertiveness, initiative and autonomy that are the foundation of successful adulthood."[3] If you truly want to invest in your child's future, then put all of your energy toward learning how to love them well. That means taking an honest and analytical look at a pair of emotions that keep us from loving unconditionally: pride and shame.

Randomly scrolling through social media the other day, I stumbled across a "proud parent" post. Those sorts of posts are generally innocent enough, but this one made me pause. It was a picture of a father with his probably ten-year-old son. The boy was holding an award, and they were both beaming. The caption read, "Back to coaching. We started the season right. 1–0. 10 points, 7 assists, 4 steals." I assume he meant the kid earned the stats, but it was the *we* in his statement and the lack of crediting the stats to his kid that made me cringe a little bit. Yes, it is subtle word choice, but what we say matters.

The sentences *I am so proud of you* or *I am so disappointed in you* are *I* statements. They express how *we feel* in that moment and oftentimes how we think those we say it to should feel. When small children hear statements like that, they don't make the distinction between what they might be feeling and what they consider they should be feeling because we, their trusted adult models, shared our emotions in that way. All the feels get mixed up, and if we leave them in that tangled pile, then by the time young children become teenagers and they set to work to appropriately untangle themselves from us, it can get really messy.

We set them up for subtle points of dysfunction in their relationships with us by saying what we may not really intend as the message. If we are aiming for unconditional love, then we want to encourage them in both their prideful moments and in their most shameful, but we have to be able to keep our own feelings out of the messaging.

Let's unpack the *I am so proud of you* statement first. My biggest disclaimer with this is that my husband and I said, "We are proud of you," all the time as our kids grew up, and the sentence in and of itself is not bad. I have been challenged to think more about the motive and timing behind that message, and I hope this chapter challenges all of us in how we approach the very complicated emotion of pride. (This is one of the reasons I've always told our kids that we saved money in equal parts for college and counseling.)

WHAT IS PRIDE?

Even the definitions of *pride* highlight the fact that it is a complex feeling. *Oxford Learner's Dictionaries'* definition of *pride* is "a feeling of deep pleasure or satisfaction derived from one's own achievements, the achievements of those with whom one is closely associated, or from qualities or possessions that are widely admired."[4] *Merriam-Webster Dictionary* also lists three definitions that boil down to respect for self-achievement; respect for the achievements of others; and, when it becomes exaggerated, self-esteem that morphs into conceit.[5] Using these definitions, I categorize pride as green-light, yellow-light, and red-light pride.

Green-light pride is the pride you have in your own achievements. Dr. Jessica Tracy, a professor of psychology at the University of British Columbia and author of the book *Pride: The Secret of Success*, has spent the bulk of her research studying pride. She would call the green-light version the healthy, authentic pride that is necessary for people to pursue and then achieve the goals they set for themselves. She writes, "Authentic pride galvanizes us to put in extra effort to succeed."[6] Anecdotally we know this. If you have ever achieved a goal you set, you earned the right to be proud of yourself. You learn how good that feels, and you become motivated to pursue other goals.

Parents who hope to help their child achieve their potential recognize that pride has to be part of the equation. Plus, there is a relational pride that exists for the parents. During an interview with Dr. Tracy, she said, "Relational pride is where you feel proud because you are connected to the person. You could feel it for a friend, you could feel it for anyone you have a connection to. Part of the self is our relationships with close others. It is a shared pride experience." Encouraging and fostering an authentic, healthy level of pride in our kids is a perfectly fine and somewhat innate behavior. The entanglement begins when that yellow-light version of pride arrives.

The yellow-light version is pride in the achievements of others. This version can be either authentic or the other type of pride Dr. Tracy describes as hubristic pride. The yellow-light pride in others is the sort of pride that can find its way into the hearts of parents, coaches, and team adult at large. It is the version that has the most potential to create dysfunctional relationships. Pride in a child's performance is authentic and pure if adults can simply admire the achievements of the kids. Full stop.

Lisa Firestone, a clinical psychologist from Los Angeles who provides therapy for families, writes, "Parents particularly express pride in their kids when they demonstrate a talent or quality that the parent values. And while we want all parents to think positively about their children, when parents make [achievement] proclamations, it often seems more about them than their child."[7] A boastful Facebook post teeters in the balance.

As soon as pride is internalized for the adult, they inch closer to the sort of pride that Tracy terms hubristic pride, or haughty arrogance. They are internalizing pride for something they did not personally achieve and take on an air of superiority or importance. You can see this sort of pride in the stands with parents and on the sidelines of games in a number of coaches. Tracy warns, "If the pride they feel in their child is like, 'My kid is the best, and the other kids are not as good,' and focusing on that comparison gives them a sense of superiority, I think it can be problematic when a parent makes it about themselves."

While watching an intense high school playoff hockey game, there was one mom I could not stop watching. She felt everything that was happening. She shifted her body with every pass and flinched at every shot. When her son scored the last-second overtime goal, you would have thought that she was the one who delivered the slapshot. She pumped her fists and then literally ran up and down the stands in celebration, hugging people as the boys did the same with their teammates on the ice. "We did it! We did it! Take that!" she said, pointing her finger at the opposing parents. "Why shouldn't she celebrate?" you might ask. She certainly can. The thing is, it was evident in her behavior that she had internalized her son's success and had quickly slid to hubristic pride.

"Hubristic pride," Tracy writes, describing a study of varsity-level college athletes, "facilitates all the behaviors needed to become dominant: arrogance, a sense of superiority, and a willingness to intimidate and derogate others."[8] Dominance is a sought-after characteristic in the sports context, and thus it is so, so easy to feel as though hubristic pride is admirable and worth pursuing. Parents who post braggy posts about their child's achievements run the risk of feeding the wrong sort of pride for themselves and for their children who watch them do it. Tracy says, "We evolved to want to get status and it's adaptive to do that. We have this impulse to make sure that we advertise our successes as far and wide as we can because it's adaptive. There is a social cost to bragging, [however,] whether it's on social media or it's in person. We don't like it when people brag. It bugs us. We find them arrogant, and so it's almost never worth it."

Unfortunately, like many places in society, this hubristic pride seems to be gaining traction in the youth sports machine. What is greatly admired in modern society is wealth, influence, and luxurious living. There is much celebration when that appears in the sports world, and it brings us to the red-light version of pride.

Red-light pride is pride for materialistic possessions and leads to boastful arrogance, celebrated in the new college sports environment, where the loudest, flashiest, cockiest, and most prideful athletes and coaches operate and find worldly success. More and more we see high school and college-aged athletes wearing bling or flaunting wealth through their cars. They say or post controversial things touting their talent and prowess. According to likes, follows, and reposts, what they are doing seems wildly popular. Don't get me wrong: The hyped-up sports/entertainment goliath is interesting, and so many of the kids are certainly talented athletes, but they present a mode to prideful achievement that does not line up with healthy pride. The thing is, I'm not sure the world of influencers and overly prideful athletes represent much of what I value most, which are balanced family relationships. They are dominant figures who could be described as having hubristic pride. Tracy argues that this sort of pride exists for high-achieving athletes, but it "can cost friendships, relationships and even mental health."[9]

Let's look at that "proud parent" post again. What if it were written from a different perspective? If the kid in the picture had posted a caption for that same photo, it might have read, "Dad's coaching my team again. We won the game, and I had 10 points, 7 assists, and 4 steals. I made Dad really proud of me." The shared moment of pride is completely familiar to people. The dad is proud to be associated with a winning team and a successful, budding athlete, and the son is proud of his achievements and that he's made his dad proud. At ten years old, the impression that something he did positively affected an important person in his life is a pretty huge deal. It becomes problematic when and if the child's pride about his own achievements becomes too intertwined with his father's pride. It is imperative to keep those threads from weaving themselves together as kids develop. We as team adult need to aim to encourage kids to have healthy pride in their own achievements and pride in the achievements of their teammates. It really doesn't need to go further than that, but in today's modern sports world, with college scholarships; name, image, and likeness (NIL); and multi-million-dollar pro contracts, we have made a societal decision that achievement warrants so much more than personal pride. We encourage athletes to do anything they can to be the proudest person in the room. We've lost control of the pendulum.

We do need kids to want growth of pride by themselves, for themselves, and not at all because the adults around them feel a sense of pride with their performance, too. We are charged with the important job of encouraging our kids along their journey, but we should be incredibly careful with pride as the encourager.

"I am so proud of you," even though it is probably true, is not the most loving thing we can say to them. The last thing our kids need is responsibility for our emotions—good or bad. Asking kids to feed the personal pride of adults can be really bad. Instead, we can encourage them by saying, "You should be so proud of yourself! Look at how your hard work paid off. I love you so much." And then when they suck, they are ashamed, they've lost or aren't playing, we can say, "You have so much grit and resilience within you to fight through this. I'm right here for you. I love you so much." You want to work toward that healthy, authentic relationship with your kids? Bring them back to the center of unconditional love every single time and no matter the circumstances!

Repetition of the call to make parents or coaches proud causes some athletes to pursue that approval above all other things. They lose track of the focus on their journey and aren't sure where their pride ends and their parents' pride begins, and the entire pursuit of sport becomes fertile ground for breaking relationships. Pride can be either a vice or a virtue. Encouraging pride in our children without needing them to be the source of our own personal pride is a delicate exercise. I think the red-light version of pride is the corrupt one. It focuses on wealth and material things, breaks apart relationships, and allows people to become consumed in selfish tendencies.

Shame

I use a video in some of my presentations that shows a dad hanging out near the net at a youth soccer game. The opponent is preparing to score a goal, and the goalie, who we can only assume is his kid, is not watching. The dad pushes the child in front of the ball that is shot, and when the kid falls down, the first shot is blocked. The oncoming player takes a second shot that goes in, and you see the dad throw up his hands and start to walk away. It is a funny clip. The emotion I think most on display in that video is shame. The dad couldn't even stop himself from letting his kid have an embarrassing, I'm-not-watching moment, and he literally went on the field to try to stop the moment that then created an even more embarrassing moment. One of the least desirable emotions we have as human beings is humiliation or embarrassment. A valuable exercise is to recognize shame when it arrives but choose love instead.

One of the hardest spots I had to occupy in the hockey stands was that of a parent of the goalie. Many parents do not realize what they say loud enough for others to hear, and even if they are not using words to express their feelings, their body language speaks volumes. My biggest personal emotional battles happened when I watched our daughter in net. Like any goalie ever, they have good games and bad games. They make great saves and give up really bad goals. Experiencing those ups and downs with her was the most work I had to do as a sports parent.

When a goalie gives up a bad goal, the initial emotion that arrives for the player and the parents cheering for that player is usually embarrassment. I had to train myself to see the emotion for what it was, breathe deeply to bring myself back to the moment, and refocus on more objective things. I'd work to see the scenario for what it was. I'd say to myself, "Our child happens to be standing in a goalie jersey, and she is certainly the last body in the way of the opponent scoring a goal, but can I change my focus to blur out the elements of the game? The voices of the other parents? To remember her as a baby? As a small person without the responsibility she is now navigating? What do I *really* hear in the comments or feel in the emotion as it waves through?" If there was not a twinge of love, then I realized I was being pulled somewhere else, and I needed to make a choice to let the feeling and anything that arrived with it pass by.

Staying in shame is a choice. The feeling of shame may arrive, but if you can get yourself centered back to love, you are making a choice not to stay there. Pride is also a choice putting either ourselves or the actions of our children first, but if we live in pride, we are not in unconditional love.

LOVE THEM UNCONDITIONALLY

Unconditional love is not hard to say, but it turns out it can be hard to display. Can you say "I love you" to your children and mean it unconditionally? Really unconditionally? It would mean the love never moves, no matter the mistakes or achievements children have. The human tendency when we are intimately connected to and companions for other people is to feel empathetic emotion. Swell with pride and shrink with shame when they swell and shrink. If all of it looked like a pendulum, then it might look like figure 2.1.

Healthy family relationships depend on the existence of unconditional love and a trust and belief that it actually is possible to achieve it. In order to begin to take strides toward the center (love), we must first define the standard on which we are building this discussion and then acknowledge that there are very real challenges to staying centered in love because of the bookend emotions: shame and pride.

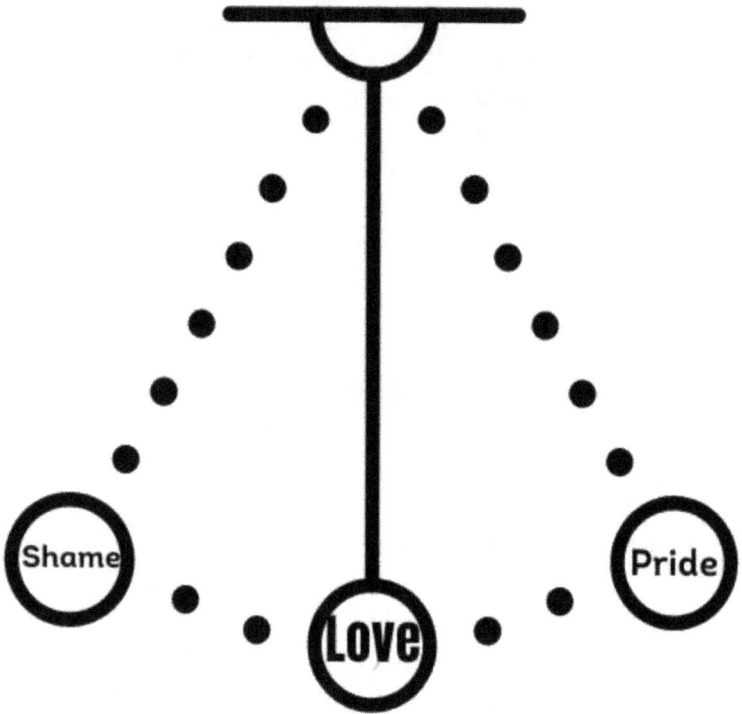

Figure 2.1. Priority Pendulum Centered in Love

Agreeing on a definition of *love* can be somewhat challenging. It is both a noun and a verb, both secular and spiritual, and it is tied to intimate emotions as well as physical expression. For the purposes of this chapter about choosing love over pride and shame, I want to lay the groundwork using St. Thomas Aquinas's definition of *love*. He writes in his *Summa of Theology* that "to love a person is to wish that person good."[10] It is the most effective way, I have found, to frame a conversation about unconditional love.

What does unconditional love look like in the youth sports context? Maybe you've heard the positive directive for sports parents to say the one sentence that means the most to their children: "I love to watch you play." It has become a movement, really, with a website devoted to blog posts, a Facebook page, a newsletter, and encouragement for parents to stay focused on this statement (https://www.ilovetowatchyouplay.com). It's a good one. It's the closest sentence I can think of that approaches unconditional love.

The challenge remains, however, in creating the tone that authentically delivers this message to eager hearts. In one of the first rounds of interviews, Jason said, "I'm not paying good money to watch my kid lay down on the ice." I think his child was four or five at the time, and he was referencing an intro to hockey. Jason's frustration was palpable in our conversation, and I do wonder if he would have even been able to pull off uttering, "I love to watch you play—ahem—lay on the ice," without a discernible tone of disappointment.

If we unconditionally love our children, then we love them while they do anything—or nothing. I cannot reiterate that enough. *Unconditional love means we love them, period.* It is not dependent on how much enjoyment we get out of an experience, like when they win or score three goals, *or* how sad and disappointed we are with bad performance or a loss. Or how embarrassed we might feel because they made a fool of themselves. Our love, if it is to be unconditional, does not swing on the pendulum in either direction. It is a fixed point to which we intentionally draw our kids back.

OK, I can hear your eyes rolling. It's not possible to keep from feeling disappointed, embarrassed, or frustrated when things are not going well, nor should we feel badly about swelling with pride when our heart on legs is running around on a field or court and absolutely crushing it. You're right. It is not possible. You won't be able to stop the emotions as they arrive, but this is an invitation to be ever mindful about the behavior you allow to be your response. I just know it is worth working through the challenge to live in the center of the swing. Always bring yourself back to center, back to love. Instead of saying, "I'm proud of you," maybe say, "I admire your effort, your courage, your resilience, your sportsmanship," all those things you want them to know you value and encourage. It keeps them and their experience separate from you and fosters the good sort of pride that they ultimately need.

I asked our grown children how they knew we loved them unconditionally while they played their sports. Haley pointed to our silent hugs after tough losses or humbling performances. Kiana said that always being there and showing up was how she knew. Nate agreed that our constant presence without pressure convinced him that we loved him and we wanted to support his passions and the things that he loved.

Dr. Tracy gave me some suggestions for how to bring yourself and your thoughts back to center: "It's about a parent being there to support them. Empathize and say, 'It does suck, and your feelings are totally valid, and it's cool you don't want to talk to me at all on the car ride home.'" It's really important, if the kid already feels like they disappointed themselves, that they don't feel like they disappointed their parents, too.

I interviewed Ken twice, and the second time his kids were on their way out of the youth sports gauntlet. He shared his changed perspective: "We laugh now when we're at the rink and we hear moms and dads talking intensely about their child's play or what programs they're in. You want to tell them to keep encouraging them, but in the end, their child will be the one to determine his or her future. They are just spectators—so sit back and just enjoy every game because it will end someday."

Kids will certainly experience plenty of both pride and shame if they play sports. They learn humility in the shameful experiences and hope through their pride. The adults riding the emotions with them need to be the fulcrum. Bring them back to the center of love with each swing they experience. When they are embarrassed, you can help them to see the humor, attain the humility, and bring them to love. When they are proud of their accomplishments, you can point out the character strength and grit that helped them to achieve that and move them back to center. Loving them toward goodness without taking on the emotions with them is the hardest and most important work we can do as their champion adults.

CHAPTER 3

There Is Crying in Baseball

Debunking Gender Myths That Hurt All Athletes

MYTHS ARE WIDELY HELD FALSE BELIEFS OR IDEAS. BELIEFS drive our emotion and essentially our emotional health. Here are six gender myths team adult needs to debunk for the sake of the children in our care.

MYTH 1: THERE IS NO CRYING IN BASEBALL

If you have not yet seen the movie *A League of Their Own*, stop reading right now, get on your favorite device, and watch it. I'll wait.

It covers all the bases of a good movie, doesn't it? (See what I did there?) At any rate, it's good because it travels the breadth of human emotion. Good movies do that. The movie is based on a true story of a women's baseball league that was formed because major league players had gone overseas to fight in World War II. Women were brought together to field teams in order to boost morale for fans. Tom Hanks portrays the drunk, has-been player who is tasked with coaching one of the teams. The line for which he—and that movie—has achieved some notoriety happens when he screams at one of the women for making a bad play, and her chin begins to quiver.

"Are you crying?" he asks, bewildered. "Are you crying?!? There's no crying!" Quivering with his own rage-filled emotions he finishes, "There's no crying in baseball!" She shakes her head no and then very obviously begins to cry.[1] It's a funny scene that plays on the gendered notion that women cry and tough, athletic men do not.

Generations of men have been raised to believe crying is for "sissies" (defined as an effeminate or weak person; an original demeaning term referencing the way a sister or girl would react). The other oft-used term is *pussy*, an even more degrading effeminate description for undesirable weakness. Both terms are still frequently used when male athletes want to mock or make fun of one another.

Emotional outbursts in sport are more acceptable if they are tantrum in nature and look a whole lot more like anger than sadness. Think chairs being tossed, punches being thrown, water bottles flying, and so on. Crying is the one behavior that has been traditionally discouraged for athletes. No matter whether it is a girl or a boy and for even the youngest of athletes, crying is generally discouraged.

And yet, crying is an innate response to all sorts of stimuli related to things like hurt, physical pain, sadness, frustration, or fatigue. In sport and while competing, crying itself is not the weakness; the weakness is in the lack of emotional control. The best athletes learn to control their emotions, especially those emotions that do not serve them. There is incredible value in emotional discipline, but learning control takes intentionality and practice. It is a problem to expect someone to stop feeling an emotion without giving them the tools to navigate it. Later in this chapter we'll review some of the tools you can use to help your young athlete.

The all-or-nothing approach to crying stunts appropriate emotional development for athletes who find themselves overwhelmed by emotions that want to pour themselves out as tears.

If someone is crying, it is most effective to determine why tears have arrived and then teach strategies for appropriate and timely control. Simply telling kids, boys or girls, to stuff an emotion is not the best parent or coach move.

Jean Davidson, a licensed practitioner with Davidson Consulting and Coaching in St. Paul, Minnesota, gave a presentation about tending emotions. She asserted that most people experience emotions when it might not be appropriate to fully express them. Using the analogy of a bucket, she explained that they place the emotion in a bucket but too often don't go back to process what they've stuffed inside. Eventually, the heavy emotional things people carry around with them have potential to arrive in dysfunctional ways and at unexpected times.

What we know about the science of tears supports Davidson's observations. The human body produces three types of tears: basal tears, the ever-present moisturizing tears that keep eyeballs from drying out; reflex tears that protect eyes from irritants like onions; and emotional tears that contain a whole host of hormones. According to Alia Hoyt, "Some scientists assert that chemicals build up in the body during times of elevated stress. These researchers believe that emotional crying is the body's way of ridding itself of these toxins and waste products."[2] Think "ugly cry" scenario.

The miraculous human body has the capacity to both store and expel toxins connected to emotion (i.e., cortisol for stress). All human bodies do this. It is right that we recognize and celebrate emotional discipline, but how we achieve that in the sporting world can result in more damage than good.

MYTH 2: EMOTIONS ARE FOR GIRLS

I was lucky, I guess, that my default emotional reaction to hurt and pain as an athlete was anger. I was fueled to rage more than I would succumb to tears. I think it was easier for me to relate to the men who coached me and to navigate the boys' teams on which

I played because I was a "tomboy" (the other gendered term that basically meant I was a girl who didn't cry).

When my sister was a little girl, her default was crying and sometimes screaming. Our backyard games generally ended with me throwing a fit and her running inside crying. When she started to play soccer on teams, at times she would cry quite dramatically. She would end up on the ground, holding an ankle or patting a knee, always with a crinkled forehead, and many coaches would go quickly to her aid.

Luckily enough, she ended up playing for a coach, starting in about fifth grade, who was able to coach her to a healthier place of control over her default emotion. When she would be down on the ground crying, overdramatically and sometimes without true injury, the coach would saunter over to her and stand near her without much fanfare. He would encourage her to calm herself down and get back up. She would eventually resolve to stand up and get back in the game. She began to understand that grit and determination are healthier responses than the drama she had previously employed. By the time she graduated from San Diego State University as a Division I All-American soccer player, she had mastered control of her emotions and especially that childhood default.

Emotions know no gender. Children do become socialized to understand emotion, often related to the gender boxes we build around them, which I talk about in myth 4. The key to helping kids with and through emotion is to recognize when they are overwhelmed. When an athlete is being flooded with emotion, team adult needs to use that as a teaching opportunity. There is a time and a place for *every* emotion, so instead of telling an athlete whose chin is quivering that there is no crying or that they should just stop, adults in the position to coach or parent an athlete through emotion should offer instead, "Take a deep breath. There will be time for crying it out later, but right now is not that time. Your focus needs to be back in the game [or here at practice]." If an athlete is too overwhelmed to continue, then forcing the issue is not the answer. Each athlete and the unique emotions they carry are to be dealt with on a case-by-case basis.

Avoiding the work that needs to happen with emotion does not erase the problem. Some people try to tell athletes to stuff their emotions while others encourage complete avoidance of those tough feelings. It is not uncommon to see rescue parents who do not like to watch their kids hurt. Instead of addressing the uncomfortable feeling head-on and talking through it or letting them work through it on their own, they simply pack up their things and avoid the experience altogether. I watched a high school senior soccer captain storm off the field after a tough loss, and his parents whisked him away without making him ride the bus home with his equally disappointed teammates. I've watched parents of a crying middle-school-aged girl huddle around her in protection, and instead of giving her tools to face her peers who had hurt her feelings, they packed up her gear and took her home. Hiding from ugly emotions just means they'll sneak up again later.

I interviewed a college soccer coach, Keri, who told me about an emotionally explosive freshman player she coached. This player regularly got carded for aggressive tackles and fouls. Keri told me, "She was a force to reckon with, and it seemed like an underlying anger she carried would sometimes come out on our opponents." One practice, the player was incredibly physical and aggressive against her own teammates. "It was getting dangerous," Keri said. "I literally had to ask her to sit out of the drill." Picking up on the cue that something was seriously wrong, Keri requested that the player come to her office after practice. The player came in with one of the captains and proceeded to explain that she was preparing to attend a court hearing the following day. When pressed for more details, the player broke down in tears and explained she had been sexually assaulted by a youth coach and was going to have to testify.

Emotions demand attention. When an athlete is overwhelmed by emotion, adults need to recognize it, be calm in spite of it, and offer a way for the athlete to settle down without dismissing or denying that a powerful emotion has arrived. It is not a decision that can be influenced by the gender of the athlete; it is a good coaching/parenting decision to connect emotionally with an emoting human being.

MYTH 3: WE DON'T PUT KIDS IN GENDERED BOXES

The world is easier to navigate when it is ordered and predictable. That means we like to think about people in terms of black or white or, in the case of gendered sports conversations, blue or pink. Changing the too-narrow roles we assign to people starts with acknowledging that we, as a culture, expect people to play roles in a defined box in the first place.

One of the latest culture wars can be seen in the passionate debate involving transgender athletes. At least half the country is in strong opposition to including people who don't fit into a traditionally gendered box. Transgender athletes comprise less than 0.5 percent of all youth athletes, yet the passion around challenging gender norms indicates how we feel about clear definitions.[3] I will not get into the debate involving college, elite, and Olympic trans athletes, but I address what team adult needs to consider when it comes to youth sports equity in chapter 7.

Cultural narratives are difficult to shift. And the blame is not just with men, oftentimes dads, for the gendered messaging children receive regarding sport. Moms and other adults certainly perpetuate it, too. In my observation, there are three levels of comfort when it comes to parents encouraging sports for their kids.

In the first level, some parents gender the sports their kids play. They encourage their daughters to participate in feminine sports: dance, gymnastics, cheerleading, and volleyball (although this particular feminizing does seem to be regional). The gendering parents really push for their boys to play traditionally acceptable boy sports: football, basketball, hockey, lacrosse, wrestling, and baseball. The second level of choice goes in line with the sports the parent or parents played. Those parents feel most comfortable encouraging their children to play the sports they know. The third type of parents are comfortable with their kids being seen as athletes of any kind. They will encourage them to try anything, including putting their daughters in bulky gear to play hockey or football and encouraging their sons to dance, cheerlead, or play sports considered to be more feminine. Sometimes it takes pink laces, a pink helmet, or pink tape on equipment to convince a girl that the sport is for her or for the girl to request the decals convincing Mom or Dad that it's OK. The message in the pink stickers is "She may play hockey, but she's still a girl."

Raising a son and daughters, coaching both boys and girls, and being a woman married to a man, I'll be the first to admit there are general differences between genders. It gets complicated when I am asked to characterize those differences along historically acceptable gender lines. Remember, I was the tomboy, so I have spent a good part of my life straddling gender expectations already. I am grateful my husband and I shared the belief to raise our kids without strict gender expectations. We encouraged our son to be emotional; to express good, bad, and ugly feelings; to sing; to try out for musicals; and to think twice about how he talks to his sisters (or mom). He's a "sensitive man" who captained his high school soccer team, positively contributed to his high school hockey team, and was the lead or supporting cast in several musicals. We challenged our daughters to be both acceptably sensitive and grit-tough. We exposed all three of our children to every sort of physical activity. Our middle daughter played soccer, volleyball, and hockey (eventually focusing on hockey), and our youngest daughter has played a little of everything and ultimately has been drawn most to soccer. Their sports journeys are unique to them, and although I note trends in their personalities that follow gender expectations, they each have a unique set of gifts, challenges, and tendencies.

The same rings true for the gendered teams I've coached. There are tendencies in the boys' teams and tendencies in the girls' teams, but to be honest, there are too many variables that affect blue-and-pink categorization. Things shift from season to season; there is change because of growth and maturation, combinations of players, and leadership from the adults who comprise those teams. An individual's responses are utterly unpredictable. I am becoming increasingly frustrated with the attempts to simplify things because, as a collective whole, we are not interested in working at it. I become especially frustrated when gender is the tool used to explain how boys and girls feel about engaging in sports. You've probably seen the quote "Boys need to succeed to feel good, and girls need to feel good to succeed." This is applicable to some boys and some girls, but some girls need to succeed to feel good and some boys need to feel good to succeed. Athletes are neither simple nor static.

Research has historically supported the notion that male and female brains have differing mechanics. Recent scientific discoveries, however, note more similarities in male and female brains than differences. Rosalind Franklin University neuroscientist Lise Eliot explains, "The truth is that there are not universal, species-wide brain features that differ between the sexes."[4] In support of that assertion, Lutz Jäncke, a professor of neuropsychology at the University of Zurich, found in a study about gendered brains that the anatomy of the brain itself is not gendered; instead, "sex/gender differences in terms of brain activations are strongly influenced by education, practice, skill level, and hormone levels."[5] Except for hormones and physical size, men's and women's brains work the same way. The environment where a child's brain is developing is so impactful that coaches, teachers, and parents can help direct the way someone's brain grows.

Hormones do affect functionality of both brains and bodies. Teens enduring the onset of puberty will exhibit behaviors connected to the new arrival of higher levels of those hormones. High levels of testosterone that teenage boys experience can create aggression and impulsivity.[6] Jäncke found in his study that, when girls and women experience high levels of estrogen related to menstruation, they also experience increased activity in their brains and more sensitivity to negative emotions.[7] Teenage girls will be affected more by experiences that make them feel badly. Each child, whether boy or girl, will experience fluctuations in hormones, and no two children will be affected by them in the same way. There are more exceptions than rules to follow when it comes to gender.

A lot goes into understanding the athlete or group of athletes standing in front of you—girls, boys, co-ed, or trans—and I contend that we hinder our ability to really know athletes when we put him/her/they in a gendered box from the outset. Take, for example, the soccer team deemed too boyish because the girls had cut their hair short. The ten-year-olds, featured in an August 8, 2017, article in the *Milwaukee Journal Sentinel* titled "No, They're Not Boys" suffered a ridiculous level of adult backlash because they were aggressive girls who happened to have short hair.[8] Uncomfortable with what they think ten-year-old girls should look like and complicated by aggression mostly attributed to boys, those young girls were inappropriately categorized and shamed. Thankfully they were coached and parented by a group willing to stand behind them, and the adoption of their motto, "Just be you," proved to be an empowering response.

People want the opportunity to be their authentic selves. Categorizing and stereotyping what that means for individual athletes is the lazy decision. Some girls feel best playing sports surrounded by friends. Some girls just want to chase a ball. Some boys are serious locker room junkies, and some boys need the chitchat to end so they can go play. It is no joke that coaching athletes is about relationships. Athletes need to feel wholly themselves in order to relate best, and that certainly means they need to feel comfortable in their own skin. That includes their relationship with gender. Plenty can confuse them, including their parents' comfort level with this conversation, their coach's ability to navigate these issues well, and the way they respond to the cultural and pervasive messaging they receive from peers and the media. Gender identity is dependent on both biological and environmental influences. It is a hot topic to discuss because there is plenty of emotion involved.

MYTH 4: BOYS WILL BE BOYS

Stop it! Old-school gendering no longer applies. My father, a hall-of-fame inductee for his high school, was the quarterback on his football team, the catcher on the baseball team, a shooting guard in basketball, and an all-conference sprinter. As a cadet at West Point, he played 150-pound football, and he boxed. He grew up in a small Nebraska town with four brothers, not far from the farm where his dad, my grandfather, was one of thirteen boys (yes, thirteen) in a family of sixteen kids. Talk about macho mojo!

My dad was of the generation where boys were encouraged to behave "like boys," manliness was a concrete thing, and the definition of an athlete was cut and dry. Athletes were boys. Generally, I think it is fair to say that my dad was most comfortable looking at the world from the "man's" perspective. I never saw him cry.

A paper published in 2020 about empathy offers a possible explanation. It claims that the gender difference in crying between adult men and women is due, in part, to socialization. "This difference starts in late childhood," the authors argue, "and likely is due in differences in socialization (for example, boys often get told not to cry, potentially leading to an inability to cry as an adult)."[9] My dad's childhood environment certainly affected his capacity for emotions as an adult.

I don't think he was ready for the arrival of three girls: my older sister in 1970, me in 1975, and my younger sister in 1977. By the time my brother arrived in 1979, I think our dad wasn't sure he'd ever be a father to a boy. I am certain he felt completely unprepared when our athletic ventures meant he had to stand on the sideline of girls' soccer games: a game he did not necessarily appreciate or understand that was being played by athletes he had never before considered to be actual athletes.

I got the sense he was a little disappointed we weren't all boys, but he never verbalized that or intentionally made us feel less-than for trying to step into the physical activity he encouraged. He tried to teach us running routes for football, threw us tennis balls off the diving board to catch, and challenged us to hold our breath the length of the pool. In the two houses he lived with us, he made sure we had a basketball hoop for shooting. One of my earliest memories as a child was when he poured concrete for the hoop he erected on the side of our driveway. I was probably two or three years old when it went up, and without knowing why, I knew that basketball hoop was really important to my dad.

Without a doubt, he loved sports. In fact, the only real way he and I ever connected, and thus a formative part of my relationship with him, was around sports or physical activity. But without meaning to, his lack of emotional expression affected all us kids. My brother's story was certainly influenced by our dad's lack of emotional presence. For my brother, our dad wasn't present much at all because he moved out of the house when my brother was five years old. It could have been disastrous for my brother, being left in a house where he was the only boy. He would have greatly benefited from the regular and consistent presence of a healthy male role model: "Research shows that without a doubt, fathers are an integral part of their sons' healthy emotional, physical, and cognitive growth from their first moments of life. Boys whose fathers love them and can demonstrate that love in consistent, caring ways have fewer problems later in life with peers, academics, and delinquent behavior."[10] Thankfully, several really good men stepped in to fill that void in our house. Our grandfather, my mom's dad, told my brother he needed to keep his room straight, so he did. Our uncles encouraged him to be active and relational, so he is. He had a gym teacher in elementary school who showed him how to have the discipline of a wrestler and coaches in high school who emulated what poised discipline looks like. Having three sisters certainly affected our brother's emotional development, but finding the right sort of male role models showed him what it is to be a good man.

Men who are good role models have emotional discipline that they are not afraid to teach to young boys. It remains a challenge for a lot of men to do that. It challenges the societal norm to be an emotional man, but evidence increasingly points to relational and health benefits when boys enjoy emodiversity: a variety of emotional experience and expression.

Socialized and repressed expression of emotion is incredibly destructive to all people but maybe most especially for boys. Psychology professors Dr. June Gruber and Dr. Jessica L. Borelli argue, "Boys grow up in a world inhabited by a narrower range of emotions, one in which their experiences of anger are noticed, inferred, and potentially cultivated." Even though people don't mean to, boys are treated differently from the moment they arrive, and that differing treatment often includes encouragement for them to suppress practically every emotion, except the one socially acceptable "boy" emotion: anger. The professors continue, "One thing is clear: This leaves other emotions—particularly the more vulnerable emotions—sorely ignored or missing in their growing minds. . . . The skills to regulate emotion are gained through practice, which boys may be less likely to have if they do not have permission to experience the full range of emotions."[11] The "boys will be boys" cycle will continue as long as we discourage emotional practice.

"Boy" behavior is not created in a vacuum. Often the tolerance for or encouragement of certain behaviors by a father or male role model can greatly influence the choices boys make. Team adult has a responsibility to open up the lines of emotional expression for everyone and with greater intentionality for the young boys we are raising. Good men need to lead this charge, and thankfully more and more strong, admired male athletes, professional football players Jason and Travis Kelce, for example, are not shying away from emotional expression that includes vulnerable tears.[12] That trend needs to continue.

MYTH 5: SEXUALIZING GIRLS IN SPORT IS NO BIG DEAL

It wasn't a conscious decision I made to use sports as my storyboard, but for me and my siblings, it was a natural fit. Both of our parents valued sports: my mom because it was a new opportunity for girls and my dad because it informed every part of his identity.

Girls in my generation who competed in sports, however, were part of what turned out to be a somewhat dysfunctional immersion into the sports world. I say that because our generation was finally granted access and permission to be a vocal part of the sports conversation, but our arrival on the sports scene challenged what many people had grown up thinking and believing about both sports and women. Gender norms began to be anything but normal. Women's bodies, in general, have been so traditionally sexualized that it stands to reason that, when they set out to use those bodies for physical activity, there was sexualization there, too. Some sports are worse about sexualizing than others.

I was a horrible gymnast for a couple years. There is a great video of me in a leotard with my underwear hanging out the bottom while I am stuck upside down in what was supposed to be a fluid roll to a handstand. The sport made me uncomfortable for a lot of reasons, but I distinctly remember consciously deciding to wear underwear. It was a coach directive to wear leotards without underwear, and in my rebellion, I willingly took the fashion hit.

The older girls all followed the coach's orders, but even then, I thought it was wrong for the male coach to mandate their use of undergarments. If I wanted to look fashionably challenged, that should have been up to me. It certainly was not the reason I was no good at tumbling. I wondered why the coach was interested in our underwear in the first place, and I was super uncomfortable in his presence without really knowing why. I was right to be concerned. I was probably eight or nine years old when I went to that gym, but I observed that the older, "prettier" gymnasts got a lot of uncomfortable attention from the coach. It turns out he was sexually assaulting gymnasts then and continued to do it, unabated, for more than a decade. It's an all-too-familiar story that continues to surface for female athletes of my generation.

The majority of the men who have been forerunners in coaching girls have been fantastic advocates for girls' and women's sports. Some of the men, however, especially in the 1980s and 1990s, had ideas, informed by their generation, about the role girls and women should play in sports. Either they employed the coaching strategies they had always used coaching boys, often negative tactics that don't work for girls, or they sexualized the girls who played for them. Both scenarios challenged self-esteem, body image, and overall experiences for many, many players.

One coach I played for used to "joke" about the bodies of some of our opponents or even when girls on our own team filled out as they slid into puberty. He would say, "She ate too many cheeseburgers." Without saying we needed to watch what we ate and keep bodies that were slim and fit, his body shaming was a perfectly acceptable banter that no one questioned. All of it certainly informed how we were developing our self-worth. Those I knew who had eating disorders were all athletes. One gymnast friend of mine became so sick she had to be hospitalized. The body-image pressure was very real.

Sensitivity and awareness are two necessary skills to combat destructive missteps. Choose empowering language, point out the usefulness of a healthy human body, and celebrate the miracles that happen when we train bodies for sport-related physical expression. Point out and fight language or destructive self-talk that can cause any athlete to think less of themselves or in a context that doesn't have much to do with sport.

Myth 6: Girls Teams and Boys Teams Can Be Coached Exactly the Same Way

To be clear, *no two teams can be coached exactly the same way* but especially when the two teams are different genders. The gender differences become more pronounced during and after puberty. (Please note: All conversation about gendered teams is in the most generalized vein.)

There are differences to coaching gendered teams, and a cookie-cutter approach is not effective. On the most general level and per my observations, boys' teams require more physical discipline, while girls' teams demand more emotional discipline. When I use the word *discipline*, I do not mean punishment as it is traditionally employed. Discipline is the practice of training people toward desired behaviors. Physical and emotional punishment is often used to coerce athletes to comply with expectations and behave a certain way. Think running laps for being late or extra pushups to get players to focus. That approach has proven successful for many coaches, but I contend punishment, in its purest form, is not the only way to encourage disciplined behavior. In fact, it may be less effective in the long run. It is possible to discipline athletes without punishment by approaching discipline with accountability and consequence instead. Because of the different disciplinary needs for gendered teams, the ways in which each group is held accountable varies.

Boys move. They love to wrestle. If there is a ball near them, they will throw, dribble, or kick it and often as high or as far as they can. If left to their own devices, they can exhibit undisciplined physical behavior. I struggled the first year I coached boys because I didn't have their physical attention. I would have the group gathered to receive instruction, and while I was talking, a ball would randomly roll through the group. Without a filter for self-control, boys are easily distracted. Eyes can be quickly drawn to movement away from a coach trying to instruct. Most of them are not trying to be disrespectful; they are just physically undisciplined. It was not something I had ever dealt with having coached girls and women.

My assistant coach suggested that, when I needed to address the group, I should line the boys up shoulder to shoulder with hands behind their backs and put the soccer balls behind me. He had seen it at a high-level camp, and once we adopted that strategy, it became a great way to regularly practice physical discipline as a group.

Discipline does not have to include physical punishment. The long-held tradition of physical punishment for every mistake, failure, or misbehavior is not a strategy I use. I am not a yeller, and it would be inauthentic if I were to try. Physical training is used for the purpose of increasing fitness levels for playing and strengthening where muscles need to be stronger but never as a punishment. Although physical punishment may yield short-term responses, it damages an athlete's overall relationship with physical exertion. The Society of Health and Physical Educators (SHAPE) published a statement to that end in 2021. Based on research and best practices the statement reads, "Administering or withholding physical activity as punishment is inappropriate and constitutes an unsound education practice because it inhibits the development of a positive attitude toward physical activity."[13]

Girls' teams demand more emotional discipline. Girls will stand still while they are being instructed, they will take physical information and put it to work right away, and they have pretty good control of their bodies. Very few of them need physical discipline at the level most guys do. Girls do have more challenges to remain disciplined with their emotions, however.

You'll hear people say, "Girls' teams are more dramatic," "Girls are more sensitive," or "Girls' teams have cliques." In the general sense, all of that is true. What those statements tell me about particular girls' teams is that they might be struggling more with emotional and relational discipline.

Girls are generally wired for empathy and collaboration, and they have a deep desire to belong to a group. Some of that behavior is innate, and much of it develops as they are socialized. The complicated wiring of girls is further complicated when the social need to belong is thrown into a competitive environment. In team environments where girls are expected to compete with one another for playing time and, as they get older, aggression is valued, it can be hard to navigate the effect a competitive environment has on the varied emotional and relational wiring of the girls or women on a team.

In my experience, the girls who struggle the most are those on teams that try to adopt a more hierarchical (or "guys") approach. Often following a player's strong personality or the coach's lead, the best players are given preferential treatment, and those players who struggle are demeaned or sometimes bullied. That strategy can cause significant damage for girls or for the teams for which they play.

It is important for parents and coaches to watch for subtle attempts at bully cliques, queen bees, and general emotional toxicity for groups of girls. Rachel Simmons's *Odd Girl Out* and Rosalind Wiseman's *Queen Bees and Wannabes* each provide enlightening looks at the complicated dynamics of girls' relationships.[14] Many of the complications highlighted in these two books can and do exist on teams of girls. With the added challenge of competition within teams for playing time and recognition, the emotional effects on some girls can be traumatic. Coaches who coach girls' teams need to acknowledge the relational differences but teach the game the same. One of my daughter's hockey teammates said it best when she said, "I don't like yellers. I want you to tell me what I did wrong, but you don't have to yell at me." I would say the majority of girls would agree with that, and there are certainly boys who prefer that style, too.

Gender stereotypes will end when we accept athletes as athletes. Prepuberty, the biological differences between boys and girls are emerging yet not as pronounced as after adolescence. The differences we see in athletic coordination for the youngest children have more to do with stereotypes and socialization than with gender. The harder we fight to change perceptions, encourage acceptance, and open up opportunities, the better off all athletes will be. Athletes are much more than their gender. Athletes need more coaching to understand and express emotions, period.

TIPS TO PARENTING/COACHING ATHLETES NO MATTER THEIR GENDER

- Remember: Human connection and relationship know no gender.

- Ask athletes how they feel (about games, practices, team experiences). Be mindful to identify your own feelings, too. Make sure you let their feelings remain separate from yours.

- Start the conversation when they are young. Remain curious instead of judgmental or presumptive. No matter their gender, they will have emotions in sport. Create an atmosphere where they feel safe to learn about the range of human emotion they'll experience. This will help them to become comfortable with the questions and to improve their ability to identify and work through their own emotions.

- If they are struggling with negative emotions, objectively say, "You seem upset. What feeling do you have right now? Why do you think you feel that way?"

- Actively listen to their responses. Repeat back to them what you thought they said, and help them identify the emotion that might be challenging them.
- Encourage them to entertain and work through every sort of emotion.
- Avoid telling them how they should feel or assuming they feel as you would.

Athletes want to participate; to be emotional; to pursue aggression; and to explore expression of toughness and grit, as well as vulnerability and passion. Athletes should be allowed to grow or cut their hair, talk about their challenges, and play any old sport they choose. Relationships are what matter, and knowing each athlete on a unique and individual level is the absolute best approach. Male, female, trans, and nonbinary children and teens need team adult to fully support who they are, how they want to play, and who they can ultimately become as athletes. I explore this responsibility further in a later chapter about equity.

CHAPTER 4

Defending Home Turf

Grow Green Grass in Your Community

My husband called on his way to the Realtor's office. I was out of town, and he was submitting our final offer to purchase a suburban house on a cul-de-sac in Woodbury, Minnesota. We were sure we had landed in the place we wanted to raise our three young children.

"The house is in Stillwater School District!" he said, panicked.

"Yes, I know. It's one of the districts that feeds into the elementary school we love so much."

"No! I don't think you understand," he said. "That means the kids have to play hockey in Stillwater. Their rink is almost thirty minutes away from the house."

At the time this conversation took place, our oldest son was going into second grade, our middle daughter was entering kindergarten, and our youngest daughter was starting preschool. Because I married a hockey player, they could all skate by then, but I had not considered the ramifications of living so far from the "home" rink.

"There's another rink that's closer. We can play there," I said.

"No. They have to play in their school district," he explained.

I had a hard time understanding why that mattered so much—that is, until all three of our children were rostered on

47

Stillwater hockey teams and my husband was coaching in River Falls for the university. Because of the way district lines had been drawn long before we got there and because there was an established culture around youth hockey, the kids and I spent about as much time in the car as we did in ice rinks. Although the kids were playing introductory hockey on what would be considered "house," or recreational teams, the association, like most hockey associations in Minnesota, was the feeder to more intense teams as they got older. Recreational turned into traveling, and traveling opened opportunities to elite and selective teams. For those who progressed well at each level, they ultimately ended up at the intensely competitive high school league. Other sports have different pipelines of teams, but most sports have adopted a travel version of their teams that can make involvement for promising athletes both expensive and time-consuming.

In Minnesota, we discovered a culture of hockey that was unlike any other sports culture I had personally experienced. I would argue the Minnesota hockey craze rivals that of Texas football or California baseball in its intensity, evidenced by the hugely popular state high school hockey tournament that draws more than 100,000 people each year. Minnesota youth hockey is a statewide machine.[1]

The Minnesota Hockey Association created a policy in the early 1990s to try to keep kids playing youth hockey in their home school districts. The intent was to enhance the community-based experience and to create good feeder programs for the high school teams. It worked. Minnesota boasts one of the most robust and revered grassroots sports models for the development of deep passion for the game, as well as high-end talent that ultimately stays to play for the high school teams.[2]

By 2009 the language of the policy changed from "Residency Rule" to "Participation Rule" in response to the youth sports migration and school-choice movement. It no longer made sense to require district involvement in associations when many families were crossing district lines for open enrollment in other schools. Players were able to play on teams associated with where they went to school, not necessarily where they lived. The policy continues to evolve, as does the intention of parents and savvy businesses, to create even more personalized experiences for families and their budding athletes.

The popularity of being able to choose something other than a public school for whom those district lines were drawn is changing the landscape of a lot of systems. Youth sports machines like Minnesota hockey are being forced to respond. Parents can choose homeschool, virtual school, private school, charter school, academy, or any other hybrid educational offering for their children. That reality will continue to tear at the fabric of the intent of the original residency rule. Fewer and fewer people play, work, or go to school in the same place where they live. COVID sped up community dissolution, but it had already begun before 2020.

Eric Higbee, a landscape architect and author who writes about place-based communities, wrote, "Sweeping changes, such as increasing affluence, mobility, choice, technology, and transformations of our cultural and built environments, have shifted our social routines and our calculus for where we invest our finite pool of social energy."[3] He was responding to thoughts Marc Dunkelman proposed in his 2014 book *The Vanishing Neighbor: The Transformation of American Community*.[4] In this book, Dunkelman argues that American culture historically has included participating in what he describes as three concentric rings. The inner ring is comprised of our most intimate familial relationships and close friends. The outer ring is for large group connection, what Dunkelman terms *ephemeral relationships*. Think aligning with other fans of your favorite professional team. The middle ring is what Dunkelman argues is disappearing. Higbee describes those "middle-ring relationships: people with whom we are 'familiar but not intimate, friendly but not close.' These relationships are typically with people in our neighborhood or town. For example, the neighbor you regularly bump into on your dog walk, fellow PTA or church members, or the barista who serves you coffee every Sunday."[5] They are the relationships we aren't always able to choose, but we are more and more able to avoid, especially if we have the means to do it.

The Pressure of Hubs

It is important to note that our Woodbury house was the sixth house we purchased, the eighth time we had moved, and in the third state in which we had lived. I hadn't started intentionally researching for this book, but I had already made observations about the various communities where we had lived.

Woodbury is a thriving, affluent suburb of the Twin Cities that, when we moved there in 2008, was home to a little over 56,000 residents. By 2021, the population had significantly grown to 77,000. Our "home" school district of Stillwater is also a booming, affluent, and growing community.[6] The sports facilities available in both communities are among the best I've seen anywhere. Acres and acres of every type of indoor and outdoor sports field, indoor and outdoor ice rinks, recreation centers, tennis courts, gyms, pools, bike paths, tracks, you name it. If there is a sport you want to pursue in that part of Minnesota, you have ample resources to do it.

For ease of identifying these high-end sports communities, which absolutely exist in places all over the country, let's call them hubs. Hubs are the places where big tournaments are held, college coaches go to recruit, families move for such amenities, and youth offerings are plentiful. As a general rule, they are the home areas of affluent people. It seems reasonable that facilities of that type only exist because of capital to create them.

There is a price to pay for children to be part of youth sports teams if they live in hub areas, however. The pressure to do all the right programming, make the right teams, travel to the right places, get instruction by the right coaches, and keep with the pace of those families near you who are going faster or doing more is a real thing. I ran across more people in hub areas with fear as their dominant emotion. They were afraid of a couple things: making the wrong choices for youth sports involvement and that their child would not be good enough by high school to participate in varsity sports.

They were not wrong to observe the heightened competition in hub areas. Traditionally hubs have more people competing for fewer spots, especially by the time kids get into high school. Because of this, political maneuvering begins in youth and usually remains impactful all the way through secondary school. Over and over, I heard parents lament about how "political" the youth sports world is. Whether it is real or not, the perception is that it's important to know the right people and to push your way into the right experiences, and the better you are at that sort of maneuvering, the better chances your kid has to have the experience you want for them. Even if associations in hub communities work hard to be objective and neutral, the perception of the people they serve often creates the political environment anyway.

One hub family I interviewed told me they wanted to stay out of travel sports programming because they had other priorities for their family and they really didn't want to engage in the politics. I interviewed them again seven years after our original conversation to see how that decision played out for their kids.

"The decision to have the kids not play traveling competitive sports has mostly worked out," they wrote in an email. "Although it hurts when they get to high school because they are not playing at the level of the kids who did play on competitive traveling teams." The kids were playing, just on lower-level high school teams. They did not regret their initial decisions, but they did end up committing to a few more travel team experiences to give their daughters more opportunity to compete better with their high school volleyball teammates.

For those considering the expense and the stress of involving children in the travel sports world, if you live in a hub, be assured your children will still have an opportunity to participate; it just might not be at the highest level. For those who do decide to dive in completely to the youth sports commitment, know that there is no guarantee for that decision either. Another hub mom I interviewed talked candidly about how things went for her highly committed football- and baseball-playing son.

"There were some things out of my control that I didn't love," she said. "I was not happy with the behaviors of parents and coaches, but we signed up for high-level programming, and it seems to be what we signed up for. There are always those kinds of people but more of them at that level."

When involved in the consistently spinning wheels of hub youth sports, there is not much time for reflection or big-picture analysis. Scheduling, traveling, maneuvering, and preparing for that next season takes a lot of family resources. It is easy to get caught up in that momentum, but I challenge even the busiest of sporting parents to consider their position in whatever kind of community they occupy.

WHAT GOOD IS HOME-TEAM ADVANTAGE IF YOU'RE NEVER HOME?

Hub communities are the drivers of travel and youth sports tourism. They have traditionally offered the destination cities for large youth tournaments, and they populate a high percentage of the travel teams who reciprocate such tourism.

The money invested in youth sports has been growing for decades, and much of that growth can be attributed to the inclusion of travel as part of the experience. In the early 2000s, the youth sports industry was estimated to be worth a little over $7 billion. By 2017, American families were spending $15.3 billion each year, and by 2022, that number rose to an estimated $30–40 billion spent on children's sports activities annually.[7] According to Project

Play, the "average youth sports parent spent $883 on one child's primary sport per season."[8] Some families reported spending up to $20,000 on one child over the course of a year.

Corporations began investing in the lucrative youth sports market about 2010. It prompted corporate and municipal investment to hedge bets by building megahub sports complexes in communities all over the country. Facilities like ESPN's Wide World of Sports Complex in Disney World, Florida; Grand Park in Indiana; Sports Force Parks in Vicksburg, Mississippi, and Sandusky, Ohio; the Future Legends Complex in Windsor, Colorado; and Rocky Top Sports World in Gatlinburg, Tennessee, are a few of the goliath megahubs. Unfortunately, for those communities banking on megahub facilities to bring in huge tourism dollars with youth tournaments, they may have miscalculated. A recent study revealed, "Parents who travel with their kids to compete in regional sports tournaments tend to be too focused on the competition to turn them into family vacations and spend like tourists."[9] It is a gamble to bank on what is ultimately a finite pot of financial resources for sporting families, and we have to acknowledge that creating this environment shuts out entirely too many people who cannot afford it. Project Play explains, "Children are having different sports experiences based on money. Parents in the wealthiest households spent about four times more on their child's sport than the lowest-income families."[10] For those who cannot afford the price of high-end programming, there is gross inequity.

"Who cares?" you might say. Sports are competitive. Life is competitive. We work hard to live and play in our hub community, and we live in a time when travel to gorgeous youth facilities is possible. No one can deny you that right. I just challenge you to think about how your work in that part of the big picture affects the other parts of the big picture serving (or in most cases not serving) hundreds of thousands of children. Beyond that and back to the disappearing middle-ring of community, if you are commuting, then you do not have time to create, foster, or enjoy the nourishing offerings of those types of relationships—and neither do your children. Nothing kills community like commuting.

Compounding the youth sports travel decisions is how the choices we all make affects the climate changing around us. The United Nations released a policy brief in 2022 titled "Addressing Climate Change through Sport." It said,

> There is an increasing acknowledgement of the connection between sport and climate change as sport both affects and is affected by this crisis. . . . The carbon footprint from transportation to/from events, the construction and use of various sporting venues, and the supply chains for sport-related equipment all play an important role in affecting the world's climate.[11]

The report mainly addresses the impact of professional sports programming, but travel by plane is travel by plane, and the emissions are no different if the bodies in those planes are ten-year-old amateurs or twenty-five-year-old professionals.

Another way the affluent sporting parents are engaging is by sending their children to highly acclaimed boarding schools or academies. I know parents want to give their kids the best of what they can afford, but just because they can afford an IMG Academy–type experience doesn't mean that the cost we all pay for that decision is worth it. People have a right to choose that investment, but the investment might go further if it were put into their communities or even a nearby sports-desert community. Practically any community could use $75,000 to $90,000 per year, the cost of one athlete's boarding school/academy sports experience. Privatization of sports is one of the most damaging parts of the youth sports craze. I cover more about this in chapter 7, but you get the idea.

We as a country used to care about the welfare and success of our neighbors. We have manufactured a way to know nothing about those neighbors now and have little concern for what happens when we make sports decisions for our kids. Now that even the hub families cannot stay put for perfectly acceptable competition, the neighboring communities that are either inner city or rural are finding fewer places to go and fewer people to play with.

RURAL OR INNER CITY OR ANY COMMUNITY THAT IS NOT A HUB

We eventually made a decision to move back to a small, rural community in western Wisconsin. That move was prompted partially by a hockey coaching job for my husband, partly because we had previously called it home two other times, and definitely at the behest of our children, ages thirteen, eleven, and eight by then. The kids were all old enough to verbalize their desire to be in a quieter, slower-paced, less-complicated environment for school, social activities, and sports. We knew they would be right about the pace of life, but we also knew it was not the decision most sporting families would have made.

Serious sporting families, especially those with resources to move where they want, often go where the sports teams are better, the number of athletes are higher, and the opportunities are greater. We looked forward to having a community into which we could invest and connect. We have one rink in our town where everyone in our house practiced, and they played all their home games there, too. I hadn't really considered that what that meant was, if one kid was playing at home, then likely the other two, as well as the team my husband coached, were all on the road and often fifty to one hundred miles in different directions. It actually wasn't any easier than the Stillwater craze; it was just different.

Since moving to this rural area in western Wisconsin, population 16,000, we have enjoyed the growing connection with community members we see in every aspect of their lives. We run into people in the library, at the market, in town, at church, and of course in the sports facilities. We have enjoyed what that community feel has provided, but I've noticed efforts within the community that disrupt what is so lovely. I have watched three separate sports board presidents of two different organizations work tirelessly to change the unchangeable about our little community. They have all been well-meaning, intelligent, and highly resourced men who see what the big communities do with uniforms, travel, camp opportunities, and experiences. They wanted to provide those sorts of sports experiences for their children and their children's teammates.

The trouble is, without the human or physical resources those larger communities enjoy, it is not possible to create the youth sports environments these men so desperately wanted for their children. They initially went outside the community for camps, off-season teams, and specified training, even inviting other families from the community to join them, but ultimately, all three families have since moved to different, bigger organizations housed in hub communities. Many families abandoned the out-of-town programming idea, and their kids stopped playing. What they left in their wake was a more anemic version of what had once been a robust, community-focused effort.

I don't blame those dads for trying to bring big youth sports opportunities to their children. The internet has made it possible to peek into the lives of practically any stratosphere of living, and what some youth organizations are able to offer the youth in their communities is truly incredible. The problem with some rural or urban communities trying to compete with the hubs is that actual resources have not yet caught up with the desired virtual ones.

Starting when I was about fifteen years old, players began to travel to be part of our soccer team. We were a hub and the state championship club in the state of Colorado. Better talent from neighboring areas began the long commutes to be part of our team. It was perfect timing for this sort of intensity to happen for high-school-aged athletes. I am baffled how prevalent this has become with families who have children far younger than fifteen or sixteen.

I have watched and continue to watch the exodus of sporting families from our current community because they are drawn to the hubs. This is not new behavior, but it is definitely gaining popularity. If they are not willing to actually move to a hub, then they commute to play for hub clubs, or they find traveling tournament teams that only require the sports tourism commitment. The members of those "traveling hub teams" only meet up in a hub or megahub anywhere in the country where a tournament might be happening. They play but don't practice, and the players come from all over the country to be rostered on those teams.

There are potential problems for the kids who decide to commute to the hubs, too. Those teams (and especially at the higher competitive levels) tend to not focus on enhancing the entire human experience in the name of competition. Members of that elite team/community are often comprised of people who have worked to get themselves into the shared social position. The team members and parents regularly see one another as competition and not as friends or community with whom they share important life experiences. High-end team folks are of the same mindset about positioning within the teams for playing time, recognition, and eventual advancement. Very generally speaking, they are not interested in deep relationships or affiliation as much as they are interested in their own child's or personal achievement.

There is a growing awareness of the challenge of "community" that many high-end teams face. Soccer Parenting, an organization created to help support soccer parents through the youth sports journey, conducted a poll of members in 2023. They identified the gap teams and clubs face in "establishing a Sense of Community on their teams," and they are responding by creating resources and curriculum on the topic. Hopefully organizers of youth sports clubs and teams will respond positively to the growing sentiment of parents to create the sort of community people realize they need.[12]

In my experience, the more affluent and powerful the people vying for spots, the more cutthroat and stressful the experiences can be, especially for the kids playing. The chess games adults play with children as the pieces do more harm than good to the very necessary social affiliation people need as they move through life's stressors. And I'm not talking about the stressors of typical competition. I am talking about an imbalance of social priority that can lead to heightened stress that comes with engagement in highly competitive programs.

Shelley Taylor, a distinguished professor of psychology at UCLA, writes about the human need to be socially connected. Taylor argues that people not only need to be socially connected, but they also need to be *positively* socially connected. She writes,

> Once signaled, the appetitive need [for affiliation] is met through purposeful social behavior. If social contacts are hostile or unsupportive, then psychological and biological stress responses are heightened. If social contacts are supportive and comforting, stress responses decline. Positive contacts, in turn, lead to a decline in the need and, in the context of stress, a decline in stress responses.[13]

Choosing to invest all our social energy on a hostile, outer-ring experience has potential to damage everyone involved.

I spoke with Sarah in the first round of interviews. She had pulled her two children out of school, her eleven-year-old son and her nine-year-old daughter, to commute for her son's specific individual sport training in a hub community that was more than an hour from their home. She woke both kids up before 5:00 a.m. each morning so they could be at the training facility for 6:00 a.m. sessions. They commuted five days a week for individual training on top of travel to participate on a team in that same area.

I tried to connect with her for a follow-up interview seven years after we spoke, but she refused the conversation. I could not confirm with a follow-up question, but I really wanted to know how connected to community they felt. Maybe they made connections in homeschool groups or eventually at the high schools they attended, but I suspect that their decision to travel as a little family unit kept their social community network pretty small.

Contrasting the isolated and lonely experiences of those who included extensive travel in their family's sports story, I've come across a number of tight-knit groups of adults who formed their relationships in their locally grown youth sports environments. The kids stayed in the community for sports programming all the way through high school. Now, even after the kids have grown up and moved on, those adults continue to meet regularly for community connection that grew under their feet as they tended to the grass they stood on.

If your family is the rolling stone, it is difficult to build a solid community connection with those where you live. Believe me. I know this from personal experience. Sports tourism creates little pockets of traveling community, but because of the nature of how it is set up, those connections are not with actual neighbors. It contributes to deepening divides.

Maybe it is of no importance for some people whether they connect with a community, but I think it does not help combat the isolation, loneliness, and societal division that runs rampant. If we cannot create, maintain, and invest in even our youth sports communities, then how in the world will we be able to create or connect to one another in a community at large?

LEAVING TOO SOON KILLS COMMUNITY-BASED PROGRAMS, ESPECIALLY IN RURAL AREAS

About ten years ago, I watched three families on a twelve-player nine-year-old soccer team leave for a neighboring, more competitive soccer community when their children were in third grade.

I knew it then but didn't say anything. I surmised that move was going to kill all we had been working on to build a positive community-based program. I knew it was devastating because the three dads of the kids who left had been coaches in that age group. Instead of working to recruit more kids to play and encouraging other possible in-town playing experiences, they left for a bigger club with paid coaches. I get it. It's easier, but what I predicted was exactly what happened. Only one of those three kids came back to play high school soccer, and he is one of three soccer-playing athletes in his class.

The class a few years older than that one took the opposite approach. All the boys, even the most talented ones, stayed in town and built a community of teammates and families around them. Angie, the woman who coached them, invited outside coaching to come to them, organized camps in town, and kept that group of boys together all the way through high school. The relationships the boys had with one another and the parent relationships built there are still strong today.

We've seen a number of hockey athletes leave rural programming far sooner than necessary, too. It is a source of status for some people to tout playing for far-off and exotic-sounding teams. Of the dozen or so kids we've watched pack up their skates and move away, only one became a Division I player—and he left when he was sixteen.

For hub families, I hope there is a push for in-house programming to grow more than the travel programs do. No capitalist will think it's a good idea, but as an educator and a proponent of childhood and family relationship building, I think delay in that sort of sports intensity is truly good for everyone.

If you live in a rural area, you very well may run out of developmental real estate for your athletes. Hold off on leaving your hometown community for most sports programming until at least puberty, which is twelve or so for girls and thirteen or so for boys.

If you can manage longer, there are great benefits for you and the community overall.

HOW TO GROW THE GRASS IN YOUR COMMUNITY

If numbers in your sport make it hard to field teams, then it is important to get creative and find ways to draw in participants. Schedule pickup games with older kids or multigenerational teams. No matter the sport, unorganized, multiage, and co-ed competition is incredibly valuable for development. It does not have to be ultra-organized, and some of the organic sport development is valuable for pure athlete development. Maybe more importantly, it is really good for building the all-important community you, your kids, and your neighbors need.

Fight for good coaching, seek out resources to train parents, and work with others to bring in good camps. There will be time for all the out-of-town travel, skill development, and exposure once kids have hormones surging and it's verified that they really are the phenoms they seemed to be when they were small. Basically, if there is *no* way your child can get any better and they are not having fun—and after exhausting every creative and community-focused effort to foster play for their sport where they are, including an effort to build up the children around them— then it is time to look at programming in a different community.

For exceptional athletes—the ones who actually become Division I, professional, or Olympic athletes—they will run out of appropriate training real estate in every community. This happens after puberty for kids playing team sports. So many teams and leagues have populated the "elite" landscape for even younger players, and parents should be wary of spending tens of thousands of dollars for what is promised for their budding players. It is not unlike academies, boarding schools, or hybrid homeschool models, where a promise of sports-focused intensity attracts willing families. It is the right answer for some people, but I fear too many folks get caught up in the status and the sales pitch.

Motivations vary for families to buy in. Some believe pursuit of Division I scholarships is worth the investment as the kids are growing. Some people find themselves caught up in the status game with their peers and don't really want to explain making a choice that doesn't include signing their kids up for the best sports team possible. No matter the motivation, there are plenty of high-end sports programming buyers.

Look at the big picture with as wide a lens as you can use. What are the true reasons you are looking for somewhere else to play? For the teams or clubs you are considering for your kids, how many of the rostered players keep playing? Can you interview alumni of the program or current participants? It is such a big investment and a huge commitment for families to decide that sport is worth traveling or moving to pursue, so it's important to weigh the information with discernment.

Community sports for small communities and inner cities are shrinking at an alarming rate, as too is the interest in high school programming that battles to serve the year-round-athlete model. What capitalism and individual drive has created in youth sports will ultimately kill high school and community-based sports as we've always celebrated them. If we value sport for the physical, social, and emotional health advantages it offers to young people, then it might be necessary to rethink local programming to better reflect those values. I sincerely hope we can shift our priorities to create, feed, and support local sports programming for *all* kids until at least age thirteen and for all types of communities that exist in this country.

CHAPTER 5

Bribery, Fear, and Anger

The Flash-Bang Motivators

WHILE WATCHING A NINE-YEAR-OLDS' SOCCER GAME, THE BEHAVior of a little forward caught my eye. Every time the ball would roll to his feet in the goal box, he dove at it with his head. After a close call with a clearing defender, the ref called the forward for dangerous play. Because U10 fields are not all that big, I heard the kid's explanation for the bizarre play: "My dad told me I could make a hundred bucks if I scored a header goal."

Oh. That explains it. The good old bribe technique to influence behavior. There are a few things wrong with this dad's effort. One, nine-year-old kids, as a general rule, are not skilled or accurate enough to deliver chipped soccer balls into the goal box onto a teammate's head. (It definitely wasn't the skill level of these particular teams.) Two, the nine-year-old was thinking appropriately at a very literal level. And three, the focus for learning, much less teamwork, was completely derailed in pursuit of a large cash payout. Bribing as a motivator is actually ineffective, not just in this case, but also in all cases when the goal is to develop motivated athletes.

Why would a sports parent use a bribing strategy? My guess is this dad, who I'll call Bribing Bobby and who you'll see again later, had hoped to motivate his budding athlete to aim for a glorious achievement. He probably thought encouraging aggression on the occasional cross would be the outcome, but I'm certain he didn't expect his son would flop to the ground instead. In addition, I would venture a guess that he did not consider the more damaging long-term effects of employing bribery as a strategy for motivation in the first place. Flash-bang bribery does influence behavior, but it is not effective in the long-term development of motivated athletes, much less motivated people.

More than 82 percent of the more than five hundred people who took the youth sports survey listed "teaching kids how to work hard" as a reason they wanted them involved in youth sports. They also listed overwhelmingly the most valuable attribute of being a team player is hard work. Adults know motivation is key to becoming and remaining a hard worker, yet too often they employ the wrong strategies to encourage it in kids.

Why does the way we motivate matter? Motivation is the driving force behind why people do what they do. It involves all aspects of human behavior and is influenced by cognitive, emotional, social, and biological components. Kendra Cherry, a teacher of psychology and author, writes, "Motivation is the process that initiates, guides, and maintains goal-oriented behaviors."[1] Every human needs it, and adults innately desire to instill it in the children for whom they care because they know how important it is.

Motivation is a big deal, arguably the biggest deal, when it comes to setting people up for success in life. Bribing is a popular tool people use. Parents use it, teachers use it, and coaches use it. Regularly the children who are bribed to sit still, stay in bed past sunrise, or run with effort will respond to the promise of a reward when they perform the adult-desired behavior. It is an example of extrinsic motivation. Reward is often paired with its less desirable cousin, punishment. You already know how I feel about that one. Punishment is the motivator that uses fear as fuel. Kids do work harder if they've been told they can go get ice cream after the game if they score, win, or otherwise perform. They also get their legs moving faster if they are afraid they'll have a punishment of some sort if they don't. Unfortunately, neither approach creates a long-lasting form of motivation, and they can backfire gloriously.

During one youth hockey season for my son, he endured "team punishment" as the coaches addressed behavior of one of the boys. The best player on the team struggled to get ready quickly enough, sauntering out to the ice late to practice every day. The rest of the boys, who got out to the ice on time, were told to sprint punishment laps until the latecomer arrived. Logically, I understand what the coaches were trying to do. They wanted to evoke compassion as a motivator for the nine-year-old boy by giving him the power to stop the punishment of his teammates. It never worked. It did, however, motivate some of the other boys to slow their entrance so they did not have to sprint as long.

I am certainly not perfect when it comes to reward and punishment, but I've learned to use language about consequences instead. When our children were young, we would tell them, "When you work hard, the consequence is better skill, better fitness, more opportunity. When you choose not to work hard, the consequences are being out of shape, loss of touch, less opportunity." Helping our children determine their role in their own consequences has been an evolving approach and often involved letting them suffer the consequences of their own choices. For example, when our son was twelve, he really wanted to go to a sleepover the night before a day filled with games. We knew he would be up all night eating junk food, and the likely consequence was going to be a pretty horrible day of performance on Saturday. We told him as much, but he wanted to go to the party anyway. We were right. He was exhausted, didn't play well, and felt awful after the games were done. We were able to show him, not just tell him, that consequences for choices are real.

Picking and choosing age-appropriate and safe consequences for the choices kids make enhances their ability to become self-motivated and autonomous kids. James Lehman, a social worker and cofounder of Empowering Parents, writes, "A conse-quence is something that follows naturally from a person's action, inaction, or poor decision. A consequence is intended to teach or modify behavior in a positive way."[2] The "punishment" of a team is not the consequence that would have changed behavior for the late skater. Maybe expecting him to pick up the locker room after practice would have. Living through the bad decision of a sleep-less junk-food-filled night offered a powerful consequence that influenced the choices our son made after that.

There is not one decision that makes a kid motivated. It comes with consistency, an understanding of natural consequences, and a maturation to own those choices for themselves. I see too many parents and coaches assume the responsibility for the kids in their charge, and they take their legs right out from under them. From an adult perspective, they know what happens after poor planning or bad choices, and instead of letting their kids learn that for themselves, they interfere by making too many decisions for them that would avoid appropriate consequences.

One family I observed over the course of raising their three children into adults remained focused on the individual needs and opportunities to grow for each of them. Their oldest daugh-ter played lacrosse through high school, their middle son played hockey and lacrosse through high school, and their youngest ended up playing lacrosse at a Division I school. When asked which decision mattered most for their family, Tracy wrote, "Viewing their athletics as activities they choose to do because those activities bring them something positive. I hope their par-ticipation in youth sports and HS athletics gives them a useful frame of reference to consider when making decisions about the use of their time—on whom to spend it and why." Knowing this woman as I do, she entered into the youth sports journey with that mindset and regularly reflected on whether their approach was in line with their overall wish for their kids and their values as a family. It worked to shape their children's motivation and fostered a pursuit of excellence.

Courtney Ackerman, a researcher and evaluator of mental health programs for the state of California, writes about motivation, "We are complex beings who are rarely driven by only one type of motivation. Different goals, desires, and ideas inform us what we want and need. Thus, it is useful to think of motivation on a continuum ranging from 'non-self-determined to self-determined.'"[3] A child who is closer to being "non-self-determined" has little to no personal motivation. On that end of the scale, anything that gets them moving is usually prompted by an external reward or punishment (a parent bribes them or a coach threatens to punish them). At the other end of the scale is full autonomy, where an athlete has motivation to pursue goals all on their own.

Progression along the motivation scale may look like this: Kids are told to do lifting workouts. Athletes are told lifting workouts result in physical strength. When they commit consistently to good programs, the athletes begin to see their strength increase, they perform better, and eventually they begin to seek workouts on their own.[4]

It takes time and maturity to achieve autonomous motivation, so team adult does have a responsibility to guide children along the spectrum toward their own motivation, but it is best to think about it as a long-term venture. Awareness of appropriate levels of development can help guide programming that best motivates athletes at their various stages of development. The long-term athlete development (LTAD) model created by Canada's Active for Life has "7 stages that correspond to basic phases of human physical, cognitive, emotional, and social development." Young kids are motivated by joy and fun, and as they gain competence, they can understand and appreciate the impact of their own motivation as they "learn to train" in elementary school, "train to train" in middle and early high school, and then "train to compete" the latter years of high school and into college.[5] Adults can positively influence with encouragement all along, but if activity or training or skill work is forced too early or efforts to motivate are for short-term results, then kids will do what the adults encourage, but they may ultimately abandon it because they never arrive at their own motivation.

Deciding that you are aiming for a self-determined and motivated adult child should inform the consistent decisions you need to make as early as you can. Behavior is influenced by external motivators, so adults should carefully employ their encouragement, aiming to help athletes land as close to intrinsic motivation on the continuum as possible.

Intrinsic motivation is the gold standard. Autonomous extrinsic motivation is the achievable goal. That means adults encourage the athlete's decisions but let them be part of the choice. Too often the form of motivation that finds its way onto courts, fields, and rinks is the sort that lacks the athlete's motivation because the controlling adult or parent influences the behavior more than the athlete chooses their behavior. Without even meaning to, well-intentioned adults push, decide, and force kids in hopes to motivate them toward goals and not always with the best developmental decision in mind. If kids don't have a say, they won't be fully intrinsically motivated to play.

Unpacking what is ultimately a joint effort, it is paramount to think about what motivates the *adult's* behavior. If you are a briber, why do you bribe? Why does it matter to you how your child behaves or performs? Are you after the positive feeling you get when you watch your child succeed, or do you truly want to find the key to motivating them to work hard? If you make the choices you make because you truly do want to arm your child with solid motivation and the tools for hard work, then there is something to be learned about how to employ extrinsic motivation well.

Extrinsic motivation is effective, but without investment from the person being motivated, it is short-lived. It might seem like an exaggerated scenario when motivation goes awry and the result is a crawling soccer player, but it is an example of when extrinsic motivation is too tied to control instead of autonomy. The dad with the hefty purse strings motivated behavior for sure, but he was the one entirely in control of the behavior. Think puppet master. Intrinsic motivation disappears when the external reward (or punishment) is the main focus. In the case of a kid solely focused on getting his one hundred bucks, nothing else was motivating his play. There was nothing about that soccer game that mattered more to him than scoring a goal with his head. It's not the type of motivated behavior that leads to finding value in hard work, staying motivated on his own, or enjoying the game for the game.

Richard M. Ryan and Edward L. Deci, who grandfathered the self-determination theory of motivation, explained in a 2017 interview with Delia O'Hara,

> Support for children's autonomy makes for better parenting and classroom environments. . . . People certainly can be motivated externally—by money, or grades in school, or a desire for social approval, for example—but Deci and Ryan say that type of controlled motivation can actually taint a person's feelings about the basic worth of the project and undermine intrinsic motivation.[6]

They explain that the highest form of motivation is reliant on "those basic psychological needs [of] autonomy, competence and relatedness."[7]

Parents bribe because it feels like they get the desired behavior by using positive emotions connected to being rewarded. Everybody *feels* good if the parent has promised Lululemon leggings for goals scored and then it actually works and she scores! But they have also completely undermined any chance that kid had to being personally invested in purely motivated play.

There are plenty of parents who are not bribers but subscribe to hard-knocks thinking about sports and parenting instead.

Sometimes they were recipients of negative extrinsic motivation, like a yelling coach or parent when they were a child, and they understand intimately how motivating fear and anger can be. Some sports have a culture surrounding them that makes the presence of those more negative emotions commonplace.

The environments around more physical sports tend to attract kids and adults drawn to a more shaped-through-fire sort of mentality. I spoke about the flash-bang versus the eternal flame. I have watched many an athlete ingest fire as their fuel, never really having an opportunity to know if it was the wellspring flame that was at the core of who they were intended to be or a fire that was lit outside of them. On football sidelines, in loud basketball gyms, in the stands of hockey games, and more and more any place children are competing, the angry, yelling parent or coach is easy to spot. They are flamethrowers and unfortunately are tolerated well in that environment. You won't find as many yellers lining a cross-country running course, on the pool deck, or at a track. It doesn't mean there are not insidious behaviors that influence efforts of athletes in those sports, too; they are just not generally negative yellers. Adults who use negative emotions to motivate can really do damage even if the intent is well-meaning. The outcome could be success as far as the sport goes but failure as far as healthy motivation and self-esteem goes.

I interviewed one family seven years apart, and when I spoke with them the first time, their son Troy was in eighth grade. Troy was a good athlete who played baseball and basketball, but he came from three generations of high-level football players, and he was heavily involved in football, too. At the first huddle meeting, the mom was already sensing the pressure Troy was under. She said, "Our son doesn't want to be the first one in the family not to play college football."

What emotion creates this sort of pressure? At the root of most pressure is fear: fear he'd disappoint his family, fear he wouldn't live up to expectations that have been expressed or at least implied, fear of judgment, and fear of failure. And all of it was baked in when they lovingly strapped on his tiny pads when he was six or seven to introduce him to the family game. It motivated him to take part and to stay involved long after he might have otherwise. His entire football engine was built around him but never in him.

"He came to a resignation while searching for colleges his junior year," his mom told me seven years later. "He knew he could play at a D-III school, but he said, 'Mom, my career is going to end, whether it ends now or in five years. I don't want to be a punching bag anymore.'"

Football, the culture, the coaches, and the family way of life had surrounded Troy with accountability, motivation, and discipline, and very little of it had sunk in to belong to him alone. He went away to college, and because the extrinsic motivators that youth sports provided couldn't go with him there, mom told me, "He struggled to thrive. He had to come home and grow up a little before going back to school."

It happens sometimes that adults employ a method of motivation that is fueled by more negative emotions without even meaning to. This strategy can seemingly work longer, depending on the culture in which it is deployed, and for some kids, it is what motivates them the entire time they play sports. The thing is, the damage incurred by athletes who stay fueled by fear and anger can be significant. They tolerate abuse, fight through debilitating injuries, sacrifice relationships, and live in a generally negative emotional and psychological space in the name of achievement. Fear and anger can be easily internalized and often keeps the torch lit, but it's lit because they have swallowed the fire, not because it welled up from within them. It can be hard to identify the destructive internal fire because it often looks like the gentle, eternal flame.

When I coached college soccer, there was a freshman on our team who struggled to get herself into the lineup. Her focus was unpredictable, and from my standpoint, she was lacking the physical presence to be an impact player. After one of our road trips when she hadn't seen any minutes on the field, I saw her running in the dark when I was making my way home. I praised her for taking the initiative to stay in shape despite spending games on the sideline. As I told her how proud of her I was for continuing to work hard, she broke down and shared with me she had been battling an eating disorder and her addiction to running was taking a toll on every part of who she was. It was in that moment I recognized so many of my own unhealthy habits because she and I carried the same damaging flame from childhood trauma. I couldn't believe I hadn't seen it before our meeting, and it fundamentally changed the way and the frequency with which I connected with the players on the team.

Internal anger is a double-edged sword. Without it, many athletes, myself included, would not achieve as much as they do. The drive to escape upset or unfortunate circumstances creates an edge in people that is difficult to duplicate without hardship.

Mason was a high-level baseball player with talent in every atom of his body. He made it through his Division I college competition and was invited to Minor League tryouts the following year. His family, a tight-knit bunch with not much backstory, was at the family lake house for their annual fishing and waterskiing weekend. Mason showed up. "What are you doing here?" his dad asked panicked. "You are supposed to be at training camp."

Mason sat in the chair and said, "Those guys need it and want it a whole lot more than I do. I have this. I have you guys. I'm never going to be angry enough to make it at this next level."

The current mental health struggles of so many college-aged athletes could be explained partially by the environment in which they developed as young athletes. By the time they arrive on college campuses or the pro ranks, they are well past the games of youth, where motivation integration should have taken root.

Instead, they work in the name of achievement or approval because they've been too reliant on motivation outside of them.

Fear and anger can influence behavior, period. They are emotions that seem to swirl around youth sports consistently, and anger especially can be traced to attempts to influence. Yelling out of anger is essentially an attempt to affect the behavior of others: to motivate athletes, to change the call or behavior of a referee, to influence decisions of a coach. When we break it down, motivational techniques (bribing, yelling, threatening) all happen in the name of motivating others to do something we want them to do.

Too easily, we let negative behaviors and emotions persist from coaches, parents, and even athletes simply because it's always the way things have been done. There is a better way. Watch for a child's passion to emerge for the sports or activities they enjoy, and fan that flame with positivity. It is the healthiest and most effective approach to raising motivated people. Try to avoid setting them on fire. Value autonomy—let them choose, follow their lead, explain why hard work matters, and find examples for how it pays off. Tell them often you love watching them work hard, and point out specific examples of when you saw that behavior. Catch them doing it right.

In chapter 12 I cover the antidotes to the negative blowtorches and offer tools to help guard the precious efforts parents put forth to raise healthy and motivated children.

Chapter 6

Injury Schminjury

Rehab the Injuries . . . Work through the Hurts

AS A JUNIOR IN HIGH SCHOOL, MY SIXTEEN-YEAR-OLD ATHLETIC body broke in two places on a basketball court. In an instant, I went from an indestructible, confident athlete to an electric-wheelchair-riding invalid. All that had been my identity was shifted from speed and competence to seated contemplation. I depended on help to drive, to shower, to dress myself, and to even get my things from my backpack. Not a moment of it was pain-free. Six weeks of casts and doctors. Six weeks of looks and snickers from insecure teenagers. My boyfriend broke up with me. Several friends quietly slid up the stairs I couldn't use to follow them and eventually some people subtly slipped off the friend list entirely. By the time I limped myself back onto a soccer field, I had been profoundly and permanently changed.

It was a pretty horrific fall, witnessed by possibly ninety baseball players who had gathered on the bleachers for a preseason meeting. I joke in the retelling of the story that I had been taking off to dunk when I fell. If I tell the story in person, people look at my 5'6" frame and actually consider for a second whether they think I could do that. Their confusion makes me smile.

The fall broke my left tibia just below my kneecap and my left ulna in a grotesque mangling. I can still picture the disfigured arm. I only looked at it briefly, but it is an image I've never quite shaken. The next thing I remember after the fall was trying to calm down my hysterical younger sister. I shielded my arm from her as I tried to console her and, once I got her attention, convinced her to go call our mom. While she was off trying to track down a pay phone, I stood to try to walk to the training room. I felt instant pain, so I sat down again.

"I think I did something to my knee, too," I calmly told my coach. He and the trainer carried me to the training room, where I had never actually been. They set me on a table, and because the break in my arm was obvious and they didn't know what I had done to my knee, they put full-limb air casts on both of them.

By the time my mom arrived, the shock had worn. As I tried to put on a tough face, I knew I would not be able to play in the next day's playoff game. My new reality grew darker when I realized I wouldn't be going to the weekend's winter formal dance either. A small tear rolled down my cheek for the first time. A few others followed in response to the flood of physical and emotional pain, but I regained control quickly because I was too tough to cry.

They put me under for X-rays and to set my arm, and when I came to, the nurse told me a man had come to check on me and was sitting in the waiting room. Every part of me wanted it to be my dad, but I knew it probably wasn't. My soccer coach was the one man who showed up for me that first night.

My dad's disastrous visit was the next night. My older sister was away at college, and my mom was with my younger sister and brother at our team's playoff basketball game. I knew the playoff game had started, but there was no way to get game-time updates, texts, or livestreams. I sat watching the hospital TV instead. Then my dad came in.

I smelled the alcohol on his breath before I heard him talk. He sidled up next to the bed, pulling up a chair as he spoke. I cannot tell you what he said, what he asked, or how he might have tried to be there for me that night. All I know was he was drunk, and I wanted him to leave from the moment he walked in the room. He was not good at dealing with injury, and I was in no shape to handle his brokenness, too.

I was trapped. For all the running I had done up to that point in my life to get away from how his alcoholism made me feel, the one time I needed those running legs the most, they were immobile beneath hospital blankets. I was stuck alone with him and the discomfort of years of pain. I avoided eye contact, remained brief in my responses, and eventually told him I felt sick and needed to rest. As soon as the door closed behind him, I began to sob.

The sobs continued when my sister called to tell me the team had lost the game. I told her our dad had stopped by, and we sobbed together. There were probably so many things making us cry in that moment. She was going to spend another night alone in the room we had shared for fourteen years, the team's positive basketball season was over, our dad was obviously not getting better, she was heading into the high school soccer season without me, and neither of us had a clue how we were going to navigate my new broken reality.

For all the trials and tests I had faced in my life up to that point, I was on the verge of my biggest transformation yet, a transformation I didn't even know I desperately needed. How did this happen? A healthy sixteen-year-old girl does not break two bones in one fall; an injured and ailing one does.

"The timing of this is pretty incredible," my doctor said. "You have recently stopped growing, and the force of impact went through your partially fused growth plate, splitting your tibia from the knee down. The arm obviously broke on impact."

A number of things swirled in my head about being done growing and how lucky I was it wasn't a big ligament. I never really questioned whether my body had been at risk or whether there were other issues I needed to address. Neither the doctor nor my mom seemed worried about that, and our focus went directly to mobility, recovery, and rehabilitation. I know now that we should have paid attention to this pretty big red flag; actually, it was the second red flag we didn't know we should have acknowledged.

The first red flag had waved, but we put it away, thinking things were probably fine. I didn't start my period until three months after my sixteenth birthday and two months before my fall on the basketball court. My fourteen-year-old sister had started the month before I did, and I was actually relieved when my body seemed to get itself on track. We chalked up my delay to the fact that I was extremely active. I played soccer four to five times a week during spring, summer, and fall, doubling up with basketball often, and then basketball five days a week, with a sprinkling of soccer games throughout the winter.

The constant activity influenced the chemistry in my body, no doubt, but so did the undernourishment and lack of adequate hydration. I was floating through my days without any concept of how nutrition played into my physical health as an athlete. I ate dinner every night, but those meals were sometimes all I ate. I didn't eat breakfast, often choosing to go shoot free throws before school instead. Some days three chocolate chip cookies were all I'd have for lunch. I wasn't consciously restricting my eating, but I did have a rather transactional relationship with food. If I had a hard workout, I could have a big bowl of ice cream for dessert after dinner. My eating would not have been categorized as medically concerning all on its own, but in combination with my activity, it should have been cause for intervention.

There is no doubt in my mind that I suffered from relative energy deficiency in sport (RED-S; formally known as the female athlete triad). The International Olympic Committee (IOC) consensus about RED-S states, "Primary amenorrhoea [an abnormal absence of menstruation] is defined as no menarche by age 15 years."[1] Check. Bones are compromised with this condition. My energy deficiency was likely identifiable, too, but ignored because of an intense schoolwork load and significant exercise regimen. The broken bones should have caused more concern than they did.

The bones eventually healed, but it felt as though my body never fully recovered. My bet is RED-S was a part of my experience as an athlete from my junior year in high school through my senior year in college. I battled injury after injury, never seeming to fully recover from any of them. At one point, I was diagnosed with anemia and given supplemental iron. During one X-ray for an entirely different injury, they discovered I had broken my elbow at some point, too. The IOC further explains, "Athletes who suffer from long-term EA [energy availability] may develop nutrient deficiencies (including anaemia), chronic fatigue and increased risk of infections and illnesses, all of which have the potential to harm health and performance."[2]

It's taken me a long time to admit that the energetic and proficient version of my athletic self was never a part of my sports story in college. I trudged on, though, despite how frustrating and futile my efforts felt. It looked like things were going well for me, but nothing could have been further from the truth. I was doing everything I could to cover up my weaknesses and the places I felt shameful. I pursued achievement at a feverish rate. Luckily, or unluckily, depending on how you looked at it, it was working. I achieved outward success but at a devastating personal price. I was missing the vital components of mental and emotional health that could have made achieving at the highest level possible. Instead, I was a hurting unit. Much of this can be attributed to the fact I was an overachieving child of an alcoholic. When I objectively catalog my physical ailments as a kid, almost all of which were connected to physical exertion, I think it would be fair to say I was a sickly child. I think it is also fair to say my physical struggles directly reflected emotional trauma I was desperately trying to navigate.

The list of ailments is long. In elementary school I had a bout with purpura that resulted in a bright red rash breaking out on my face when I exercised. I suffered regularly with bloody noses and hives. One doctor said I must have been allergic to my own sweat. It was his only explanation for hives while exercising when exhaustive testing revealed no other identifiable allergy. I was diagnosed with exercise-induced asthma and provided an inhaler. I cheated on an eye exam, warranting reading glasses I did not need when I was in fourth grade. (Sorry, Mom.) I legitimately suffered from chronic sinus infections and headaches. The only time I could schedule sinus surgery was when I was laid up with my broken arm and leg. You should have seen the nurse's face when she pulled back the sheet to start my IV and found a full arm cast.

Given the situation at home, my injuries were likely tied to the emotional stress I was trying to navigate. Robert S. Weinberg, a professor of sport psychology, writes, "Sport and exercise participants who are experiencing major life stress or changes and who do not have good strategies for dealing with these stresses are more likely to be injured." Until writing this book, I hadn't realized the psychological warfare I was waging with my own body. Weinberg explains that humans under stress have increased muscle tension, and that tension can interfere with normal coordination, thus increasing the chance for injury.[3]

My body was legitimately injured because the rest of me was occupying an incredibly negative space. Games and sport were not fun for me. They were serious business and hypercompetitive, period. Anything less than that was for weaker people. I wanted to prove to the world and to myself that I was above my circumstances. It seemed like a constructive mindset at the time, but in conjunction with everything else I didn't want to analyze, I was not at my healthiest. Unfortunately, I didn't have coaches or mentors who challenged me to even think any other way because I helped their teams. Plus, there is a necessary culture around elite sports to push through pain. It's important for adults to be mindful about what that ask does to some kids.

Working through my sports story has given me a clearer lens to see what all those injuries did to me. Now I hope to make purpose of that pain. There was certainly grief to unpack, too, but I get to how grief shows up in other ways in youth sports in chapter 11.

For the athletic girls in your care, I would encourage in-depth conversations about the miracle of their bodies. If they are not yet using an app to track menstrual cycles, nutritional intake, or hydration, then do everything you can to convince them to do that. For all athletes, no matter the gender, they need supportive adults who care for their complete physical, mental, and emotional health. If you know something bigger might be happening for an athlete outside of their sport or if something potentially upsetting is happening in your home, then it is important to honor all the injured or hurting behavior as it arrives. The kids may be trying to communicate something they are experiencing emotionally. Healthy athletes have goals and clear boundaries and tap into the information available to keep them well. They know what exercises strengthen them, and they know what exercises hurt them. Any adult with access to young athletes needs to help kids identify and aim for goals and give them permission to set healthy boundaries.

Using the analogy of the airline instruction to apply your oxygen mask before assisting others, the emotional health of athletes starts with the health of the adults. Dr. Jim Taylor, a psychologist in sport and parenting, challenges parents to "know your emotional baggage: If you are often frustrated, angry, or afraid, your children probably will be too."[4] Parents are an athlete's best chance of achieving positive, emotional health. In lieu of a healthy parent model, other adults in the sports environment need to fill that void. Kids need adult champions to help guide them toward not only the physical goals they reach for but also the healthy emotional goals they deserve. We must take on the responsibility to help them when they are physically injured, as well as when they are "hurt."

"Are you injured, or are you hurt?" I asked my seven-year-old son when he came limping over to me after a scuffle on the playground. He had not been able to beat out the taller boy to catch the "500" toss that ended the game, and from what I had observed, he wasn't injured; he was hurt—emotionally. He was on the verge of tears, and he was starting to understand the cultural expectation around competing and emotional outbursts. Crying was only going to be acceptable if there was a physical explanation. After we left the park, he was able to share with me the source of his hurt. It was at that point we began practicing what to do when the emotions that arrive are painful.

We developed a system of language in our house. We acknowledged a clear distinction between being hurt and being injured. Hurt can be physical, mental, or emotional, and real pains that arrive with hurt absolutely need to be acknowledged and addressed, but they can provide fertile ground for growing grit. Physical injury is an undeniable injury that results in malfunction of the part of the body that is hurt and requires rest, recuperation, and rehabilitation. Often athletes assume because they are feeling hurt, they must be injured, or they default to "injury" because they no longer want to battle what is hurting them. I never want to discount an athlete's assertion that they are hurt, because if they say they are hurt, then they are hurting somewhere. The investigation, and possibly extra work, begins when there is no real physical injury to explain the hurting. It's up to the adults in the room to help them determine the cause.

If you have been around youth sports for any length of time, then you have run across athletes too emotionally hurt to compete. They pull themselves out, they refuse to go to practice, they find a place to hide on the sidelines, and sometimes they even fake real physical illness or injury because it is easier to get empathy for physical ailments than it is to admit legitimate emotional pain.

My mom was told by a doctor this would be the case. When she asked a psychologist if it was possible to overschedule us, he told her that she needn't worry because, if we were overscheduled, we would either sabotage it ourselves, or we would eventually get hurt. In microcosmic ways—and in eventual big ways—that is exactly what I did. It was not my mom's fault, but neither of us really knew how to talk about the hurts we were experiencing, and compounded by the weight of competing through those hurts, it made layering of pain inevitable.

Both physical injuries and emotional hurts need to be acknowledged, attended, and healed. Creating a language and conversation around physical and emotional wounds is imperative for the growth and development of all children, as well as for the adults who might be hurting, too. Sports offers fertile ground for those conversations.

All negative emotions, especially if they overwhelm us or remain unattended, can cause damage. Essentially anything that evokes emotional distress can be described as the pain we feel when there is not a physical source to blame. Feeling hurt can happen instantaneously, or it can be caused by emotions that you've avoided dealing with, like anger, sadness, shame, guilt, and anxiety.[5] The stress hormone cortisol shows up for all of this.

Psychologist Elizabeth Hartney writes, "Ongoing stress may cause the physical effects of emotions such as fear, anger, and sadness to linger far after the event that triggered them has ended. When this happens, what once were natural, healthy emotional responses to a singular event can now have a negative effect on our lives."[6] When cortisol remains in our bodies, we can suffer all sorts of physical ailments, including diarrhea, dizziness, headaches, loss of appetite, fatigue, muscle pain, nausea, pain in the arms and legs, and stomachache or gastrointestinal issues. The emotional weight can sometimes manifest physically, and the human response ultimately leads to behavior meant to dissipate the pain. Sports intensity can provide distraction and an outlet for hurts we carry; however, if emotional pain exists, then that pain must be processed to regain full health.

Depending on the environment, if emotionally hurting adults are in an emotionally charged gym or surrounded by other emotionally hurt adults on the sideline, then when an injustice happens (bad ref calls), their child is subject to unfair playing time, a dangerous play happens that puts their kid at risk, or embarrassment takes hold because their kid absolutely sucks that day, emotional outbursts can happen. It comes in fights, brawls, bullying, and angry comments. The human heart can only handle being inundated with ugly emotions so long before an outburst is inevitable.

No one walks into a gym planning to go batshit crazy, but maybe we should get better at expecting we'll feel the feels when we're there, and if we're carrying crazy, angry thoughts with us, then we have the potential to be the powder keg that sets other crazed-feeling folks into motion, too. It's everywhere and unfortunately often tied to dysfunctional handling of overwhelming emotions that have been buried by denial and distractions or accompanied by response behavior that never developed well at all.

Hurtful words in bullying or taunting because of mistakes or failures, as well as being embarrassed, ghosted, or isolated, are just some of the ways people are exposed to hurt. Perception is reality, and I've learned there is not much difference between what may be absolute truth and what people believe to be true. What you think hurts, hurts. And if it hurts, then you *must* take the time to work through it. Unattended hurts never really go away.

During huddle interviews, buried emotions would sometimes surface. When Krystal was telling me her sports story, she became emotional. I could see the pain on her face, and I could feel how long she had held it. She shared with me that, as a preteen, she ran track but remembers distinctly why she gave it up early. A middle school coach said to her, "You're gonna have to run a lot faster if you want to be like your sister." Her sister was eight years older than her. With a shaky voice, Krystal said, "I was done. He might as well have slapped me in the face." It was the beginning of her sad relationship with sports. "I didn't do anything in high school because I had no desire, and I believed I would not have skill enough to play. I did not have good self-esteem." The words of that coach, whether intended or not, lingered into high school for Krystal, but because she hadn't really found a way or a reason to work through how hurtful that was for her, she was still hurting when I interviewed her two decades later.

Instead of honoring the tears, the frustration, the ways a person is trying to communicate emotional pain and helping them to work through it, people become cut off from the practice and never move past that point. What parents and coaches say is much more impactful than we might realize. And it's important to recognize that the sensitivity of each child varies. Emotions, or rather the behavior we use to express emotions, takes practice—for all of us.

When our youngest daughter was about ten, she had been selected for an Olympic Development Program (ODP) soccer team that trained about an hour away from our house. My sister and I had been part of this program as young players, so I knew the opportunities this might open up for her. She had gone to a few of the training days, worked hard while she was there, and was doing well. One Sunday afternoon, I told her to get ready to head to practice. She yelled up from her room that she was not going to go. She was using a resistant voice we had heard before. She sounded like that when she did not want to get on the bus to go to school or get out of the car to join a hockey practice late. Up to that point, her resistance accompanied activities she didn't enjoy as much as soccer, so her choice to avoid the ODP practice was surprising. It was also incredibly emotional for me.

I fought with her to get her upstairs and to get her bag packed, employing every (extrinsic) motivational tactic I could muster. Eventually I got her outside the house, and as I was loading into the car, she took off running down the street.

I followed our distraught daughter in my car as she sprinted away from me, and all I wanted to do was make my own feelings of embarrassment, shame, and guilt go away. I figured getting her to agree to go was the best solution. I cajoled, I convinced, and I eventually got her seated in the passenger seat. We drove in silence for an hour, now pushing against the time that would make her late to the session (the most anxiety-inducing thing on the planet for her). When we arrived, she had about five minutes to get her stuff on, but as we sat in the parking lot, something else paralyzed her, and she refused to finish getting ready. We sat for the beginning of the session and for the first fifteen minutes, until I accepted that she was not going to play that day. I pulled out of my parking spot, and we drove home. That was her last experience with ODP. It was also the point we began a rather lengthy road to diagnose, then treat, extreme levels of social anxiety. She was so obviously hurting, but I was still hurting at that point, too, and I wasn't seeing, listening, or observing clearly enough. I wasn't helpful; I was actually part of the problem for a while.

I know that episode was impactful for both of us. Living with the constant mantra of choosing to grow meant I had to take a long, hard look at how I was showing up, not only for my own kids, but also for all the kids for whom I had the privilege to coach. That might be why I have landed on coaching high schoolers. They and their parents have the most to teach me. High school is the time when the emotional rubber hits the proverbial future road. Teens and parents collide in their shared and unique emotional challenges, and it is where coaching feels most purposeful for me.

EMOTIONAL GROWTH TAKES PRACTICE—AND A SAFE SPACE TO DO IT

I try to do regular check-ins with the players on the teams I coach. My prepractice question is "How is everyone feeling?" Sometimes they'll talk about physical aches and pains, but I constantly work to gain their trust enough that they will also share with me how they are feeling emotionally. I listen for them to tell me they are nervous, anxious, excited, exhausted, depleted, sad—you name it. One of the most beautiful things we can share with another human is the range of emotions we get to experience. In a position of coaching or parenting, I try to help the kids learn to acknowledge what emotion has arrived and, instead of controlling them (which feels like suppression), encourage them to process appropriately and then gain discipline of the behavior response. That's emotional maturity.

Freshmen and sophomore girls cry (with practically every emotion). Chilling out the parents who are maybe not sure how to interpret this extraordinary moment of emotional growth is an added challenge. They are feeling hurt and cannot necessarily verbalize why, so I try to simply come alongside them to let them know I am cheering for their efforts to work through it.

High school boys have outbursts. Testosterone is a new hormone evoking a high level of emotion they have not yet learned to manage. Hurt manifests as aggression and yelling and usually involves some sort of physical release. Often boys have been taught to express every emotion that arrives with a level of machismo. Dr. Kevin Chapman, founder of the Kentucky Center for Anxiety and Related Disorders, writes, "Boys are taught hyper masculinity and don't express emotions. It's been suppressed. I don't think we've done an adequate job of equipping coaches to handle these conversations. There has to be a safe environment for young athletes to vocalize they're struggling with nerves."[7]

Tips to Help Hurting Kids

- Spend time attending to your own places of hurt.
- Pay attention to warning signs. Chronic illness or injury could be a sign of emotional distress.

- Teach them the difference between being hurt and being injured.

- Honor their energy levels, and choose programming that aligns.

- Carve out time each week, each month, and each year for rest.

- Employ emotions coaching. Identify the emotion, feel and work through the emotion, then choose the appropriate behavior.

- Seek professional help if you do not have the tools to address your needs or the emotional needs of the children in your care.

CHAPTER 7

Level the Playing Field

Embrace Real Inclusion despite All Our Differences

YOUTH SPORTS PROVIDE THE OPPORTUNITY TO ADDRESS SOCIAL inequities, even if we don't feel like it.

Before taking the ice, the room was filled with tension. There were silent tears, migraines, upset stomachs, throwing up, pale faces, wringing hands, and chest palpitations. You would think I was observing the scene of pregame jitters for an Olympic gold-medal game, but this happened in a locker room prior to a U10 girls' hockey tryout. U10, meaning the girls were eight and nine years old. The parents and the girls were all exhibiting extremely high levels of anxiety and fear.

What exactly was the precipice of this emotion-filled moment? Before the teams were even created, the players (but, I would argue, even more significantly the parents) were anticipating the potential for negative feelings associated with exclusion, undesired and assigned status, and potentially perceived injustice. Three leveled teams were going to be created out of the skaters in that room, and for varying reasons, each person worried about how the budding hockey player would perform and thus measure up: A, B, or C. Everyone knew that the divided teams afforded disparate experiences. The A teams had different swag, more tournaments, and better travel options, and let's be honest, all players and parents want to say they made the A team.

The parents were probably nervous about those things, but they should have been more nervous about labeling their young daughters something that could and would be interpreted through the brain of a nine-year-old concrete thinker. Children that age are quite influenced when you tell them who they are, and it doesn't serve them no matter what letter you give them.[1] I stood in the locker room glad I had told our daughter it was just another hockey practice. I wondered why the adults tying their daughters' skates were willing to engage in a system that could cause such a scene. Children would never orchestrate something like that. Only adults would.

We are wired to want to make the A team. There is plenty of evidence suggesting we are highly competitive about achieving not only high status but also higher status than others around us.[2] We position ourselves and our children to occupy the highest rung on the status ladder we possibly can. Status used to be measured in house size or car brand, which of course it still is, but status is also evident in the youth sports arenas. We cannot seem to help ourselves. Modern parenting is trending toward increased investment in children: emotionally, psychologically, and financially. Today's parents defend increased and sometimes total investment in life outcomes for their children.[3] It is how we can prove we are the best parents around. Where our investments go, there, too, go our emotions.

Emotions swirl around tryouts, team placement, equal playing time, and discrimination. The greater the fight for status, the greater the feelings of injustice or inequity arrive, and the hotter the tempers and emotions become. When adults try to mitigate negative outcomes for status-labeling experiences, they use their finite energy to do what they can to ensure their child receives fair treatment or some sort of advantage instead of doing anything to revamp the system altogether. Additionally, the competitive nature of team sports pushes back against the very idea of equity. Competing for resources, for spots on teams, and for wins is the bigger game overarching all that happens in the youth sports world.

We are indeed a complicated species, however. At the same time we pursue societal status for ourselves or our children, we also abhor injustice. We are wired to seek justice, and Melanie Greenberg describes, "We seem to have a happiness response to fair treatment and a disgust or protest response to unfairness."[4] Navigating youth sports can be exhausting as we pursue both status and equity. What if instead of either/or, it could revert to yes/and?

When I was a young club coach for an elite travel team, I recognized a shift happening from team to individual. On a trip to a regional tournament, the girls struggled in their first game because a few of them were more concerned about how they individually performed for the college coaches who had come to recruit them. I spent the rest of the weekend trying to convince them they would actually show better for the coaches if the team did well. Elevating everyone in the name of team success still allows for people's gifts to be highlighted.

Of the five hundred people I surveyed, 84 percent believed that "political power in youth sports can determine the athletic path for an athlete," and 79 percent "think parents try to manipulate their children's sporting experience too much." Adult influence swirls like an ominous cloud above the youth sports endeavor, yet we keep allowing situations where small children sit on the verge of breakdowns. I'm not sure we should be satisfied that we are doing our team adult job very well. Instead of manipulating or politicizing the youth sports environment, we should pool our collective energies to create experiences to better serve all kids in the name of equity (something 88 percent of those polled believed we should). Choosing a new route of equity will certainly benefit all children in the long run, including our own.

EQUITY

We have two dogs in our house. One is a ninety-eight-pound yellow lab; the other is a fifteen-pound chiweenie. I practice equity in their care. I make sure they are both fed, and they each get their exercise, even though one eats much less and walks instead of runs. Equality is giving each of them the exact same things. Equity is giving each of them exactly what they need.

As it applies to youth sports, equity is providing every child regular opportunities to play in a safe space, guided by trusted adults, and with the use of quality equipment. Equity is about attending to all voices the best we can, starting with the voices of the children who live in our own homes.

FAMILY EQUITY

We cannot attempt to address the issues of societal equity if we are unwilling to determine how equitable our own family units are. Every house filled with more than one sporting child has the potential for what I term *shadow children*. You know, shadow children are the kids who are dragged to the sporting events of their siblings, often seen scrambling up bleachers or hiding beneath them. Sometimes those kids get their own shot at youth sports glory, but sometimes they are relegated to the role of eternal cheerleader for their spotlight sibling.

Psychologists have a formal term for these sidelined children: the *disfavored sibling*. According to a compilation of studies, disfavored siblings are those children who either receive or believe they receive less attention from their parents. It is a state of mind connected to parental differential treatment (PDT): "Children are sensitive to PDT and report that it occurs frequently, . . . and the disfavored sibling tends to show higher levels of depression, antisocial and delinquent behavior, and substance use."[5]

Some studies about sibling awareness of PDT suggest "stronger negative effects for girls than for boys and for older than for younger siblings."[6] Older sisters in shadow kid roles might be among the most challenged for negative outcomes in an inequitable house.

Most parents don't expressly admit they have a favorite child, and they may not mean to set up the dynamic where one or more of their kids is sensitive to PDT, but chances are the more children you have, the more real the possibility that one or more of your kids is struggling with feeling less than. It is valuable to talk with them about their perspective. Ask them each individually who they think your favorite is and why. Then listen—really listen—to the reasons they give you for the perspective they have. Their perspective may not be true, but what is true to them is their truth. The emotions around inequity happen at every level where people battle for elbow room or a voice at the table.

EQUITY CHALLENGES ON TEAMS

When I interviewed Dr. Nicole M. LaVoi, director of the Tucker Center for Research on Girls and Women in Sport at the University of Minnesota, I asked her what one thing, if changed, could improve the youth sports experience. With very little hesitation she said, "Mandate equal playing time up to age fourteen for all levels of sport, both at the recreational and competitive levels." The developmental needs of kids younger than fourteen demands opportunity to play. That doesn't matter if the kids are on a competitive team or on a recreational team. Developmentally, kids younger than fourteen don't completely understand the value of bench players other than "not valuable," and it serves all the players to learn how to be in every role a sport offers. The blog I wrote about Dr. LaVoi's comment and another I wrote challenging organizations to ban tryouts until age twelve have garnered more interest and debate than anything else I have written about youth sports. Most emotional challenges I have fielded from parents of the athletes I've coached involved playing time or team placement. People get very emotional about equity within teams. Before kids are old enough to process their participation separate from their personhood, equal playing time serves all of them. Adult emotion about this topic is the sole reason we have not been able to make that happen across the board.

Why fourteen? The average age for athletes to have completed puberty is fifteen, so having equal-playing-time mandates up to fourteen gives the space most kids need to grow into their bodies, even if it is slightly in advance of complete physical, emotional, or mental development.[7] First-year athletes in high school are usually fourteen or fifteen, so by the time kids get into high school, their maturation has developed adequately enough to understand what it means to earn playing time.

Aside from mandating equal playing time for every kid on the roster, the challenge comes in creating teams that can be equitable top to bottom. As kids start going through puberty, gaps develop in coordination, speed, strength, and technical skill. Putting like-skilled players together is very important to allow for an atmosphere where equitable playing time can be most valuable. That means—you guessed it—leveled teams work best. What do we do to reconcile the need for comparable athletes to be rostered without causing potential distress? Abandon tryouts.

When kids are age ten or eleven, it is a good time to start identifying talent and grouping by ability. I have watched some club soccer organizations do this better than others. Instead of tryouts, they let kids mix, practice, and play for about a month and then assign teams. The talent can be pooled this way to create teams where equitable playing time makes the team competitive, and there is no need for a singular evaluation period that causes undue anxiety. Then the teams can offer equal playing time to every member on that team until those kids are fourteen. Or better yet, let's create little pockets of Norwegian-style youth sports:

> Your kid tries multiple sports at the local club whether or not they're any good at them, you pay a nominal fee but only if you can afford it because it's subsidized by the national lottery,

coaches are volunteers, there are no scores or standings or regional competitions until age 11 and sometimes older, children are encouraged to pick their sports and decide amongst themselves what they want to do in practice ("Scrimmage!"), most kids don't specialize until late in high school.[8]

I do realize, these little suggestions cause big emotional reactions. Part of why this topic garners such emotion is that we as a society cannot seem to acknowledge that someone else's view of equity may feel unfair to us, and there are varying degrees of interest to even pursue it.

"It's not fair to make my kid suffer a loss because the 'bad' kids have to play just as much. All the kids want to win," said a frustrated parent balking about the equal-playing-time suggestion I made during a presentation. As the voice for the too-oft-benched kid and his parents, I would respond, "It's not fair to not be allowed to play, either." Entertaining all sides is the only way to achieve empathy and the only path for substantive change.

I was a coach long before I was a parent, and I was even a reluctant parent-coach at the high school level because I knew what challenges in equity I would have to navigate. I thought long and hard about applying for the high school boys' head soccer coach position. The program would include our son and was in a school and community dominated by football. I would be the only female coach of a varsity boys' team within a hundred-mile radius and didn't have much confidence that there would be support for me there at all. Over the course of the six years I coached that team, several issues of inequity challenged me.

When our son joined the high school soccer team as a freshman, my husband and I thought he would experience some of the things we had enjoyed as high school athletes. We were horrified to discover his soccer experience was going to be anything but what a high school activity should have been. They lost every game but one that season, and most of those losses were by mercy-rule decision, meaning they lost by ten goals before the full game had been played. There were ten seniors in the program that year, and they were not allowed to participate in playoffs because they had accrued too many yellow and red cards over the course of the year. I've never seen a more deflated, discouraged, frustrated, and ashamed group of athletes in my life.

The team was relegated to one season at the JV level, and then the coach left. It was on the heels of those two rough years when I was approached by a couple of my son's teammates to consider applying to be their coach. I cannot accurately quantify the level of hesitation I had about stepping up to coach them, but in the name of choosing to grow and because it was a need to be filled, I agreed. In retrospect, and after learning the uphill battle they were all fighting in the sports climate where they played, the behavior of those seniors looked and sounded a whole lot like rebellious, shadow children.

All the decisions I made as a coach were focused on trying to create an equitable environment for those athletes. They deserved to be treated with respect. They deserved to be in competitive games. They deserved to have educational opportunities in sports that were not always about learning how to lose. Long before I started coaching, every bit of energy in our town had gone into building a state-renowned football program, and it was at the expense of other sports in that season, most specifically the boys' soccer program. There was a reluctant acceptance of the inequity from the soccer-playing families, when instead they might have taken their legitimate concerns to the school administration or school board. The issues were ultimately exposed, but it wasn't the soccer families who were able to wage the fight.

The football team dominated in our conference and absolutely needed to compete there, but the boys' soccer team never enjoyed the sort of competition that makes high school sports the gem they can be for teaching life's best lessons. They were overshadowed by the spotlight sport of football in the school and community and suffered as the basement-dwelling shadow program in the conference.

A number of very good soccer players chose to run cross country instead of playing soccer. A mother of one of those runners told me directly, "He doesn't want to play soccer because he doesn't want to lose." Changing the cycle needed to happen with more equitable competition for the high school team, but without a way to play more comparable opponents, it was an uphill fight.

A couple boys did end up quitting football to join soccer while I was the coach, but they fielded rude and disrespectful comments. They shared with me that they heard the football coaches disparage soccer and those who played it. Many of the football players adopted a similar attitude and then carried opinions of superiority into the high school halls, where we all know status reigns. It created a cultural inequity unlike anything I have experienced, before or since.

I did what I could do, given the situation. I wasn't given administrative support to change the conference we were in, so I tried to teach those kids to reframe what they valued. I wanted them all to recognize their worth outside of the scores or conference standings. I was constantly working behind the scenes to create equity by scheduling games with better-leveled competition, but my focus with the boys was to make sure they felt their worth just because they were there. I should mention, too, that the team was among the most diverse on campus. One season we had nine ethnicities represented. It was a strong and resilient group that had developed thick skin in most areas of their lives, and we started to celebrate each time we played a full game.

One mother I interviewed who had four boys, a pair of soccer players and a pair of football players, straddled the cultural divide every fall. "You had to cheer equally, and you had to give the same amount of your blood, sweat, and tears to both," she said. "From a parent's perspective, I didn't feel like either team did without the basics to be successful. It was more the intangibles that were not even." Ultimately, three of her boys went on to play at the college level for their sports, two Division I football players and a Division III soccer player. When I asked her if there was anything about their high school experiences she would have changed if she could, she said,

> The football players had a very positive experience that made them better people. The soccer players, I think the same, but I would have wished they could have had more soccer players to give them an opportunity for success. I think they became better people because it wasn't easy, but I think they missed out on some of the confidence gaining they could get from success, like the football players had.

Equity would have made a difference.

It was only when there was a Title IX investigation launched against the school district that I began to think things might change for those soccer boys. Title IX, an amendment of higher education, has been most effective in driving sports-experience equity. The amendment was adopted in 1972 and has allowed a new generation of parents—mothers and fathers who were raised under Title IX—to embrace athletic opportunities for their daughters. Title IX doesn't cover all inequity, however.

The complaint was filed in September 2017.[9] It illuminated the special treatment the football team had received for decades, but the lens of equity that had to be used to challenge that status quo was gender. Despite real disparities between the football program and the soccer program, there was not a similar vehicle to point out those inequities as they applied to two teams of boys. A federal investigation ensued.

It seemed the culture made it difficult for anyone who was not on the spotlight teams to feel fairly treated. Following the investigation, a resolution was created to address the noted disparities, and it was signed in September 2019.[10] Many of the resolved issues were slow to implement because of COVID, but I can attest to the many equitable changes that have happened as a result of that complaint and investigation. One of the most marked changes has been in the weight room. The room that had been used nearly exclusively by the football team was completely renovated and staffed with a strength and conditioning coach who works with every athlete in the building.

Favored players and favored teams are like the favorite child. Sibling relationships are harmed in a family with parental preferential treatment, teammate relationships are harmed on teams if the coach plays favorites, and entire groups of people can suffer when they begin to believe that they don't matter as much as others. I asked my daughter Haley, who participated in a panel during the Title IX investigation, what damage she thinks is done when there is varied treatment among teams. She said, "I think there starts to be a confidence issue. Teenagers are trying to figure out who they are and (in not so many words) they are being told they don't matter as much. It hurts their self-esteem." Adults have the power to change that narrative and building up the self-esteem of every child or teen is always a good thing. Title IX was an effective vehicle to challenge what seemed inequitable. Without it, there might not have been any change at all.

EQUITY THROUGH LEGISLATION
During one of the huddle interviews, the participants became passionate about equity and affluence. Christina said, "Sports are for wealthy parents who want to outsource that part of their parenting." The group agreed and pushed the conversation toward what could be done to create equity.

"That's only going to happen with laws," Mike argued. "People are not going to change unless they are forced to."

I was likely too optimistic and naive at the time of that conversation. I believed people with means would be happy to create opportunities for those who are not capable. After watching what has developed over the last decade, I think Mike might have been right. People who have the means to pay to play with the best clubs, afford the most expensive training, and travel to high-end tournaments have continued to do that. They have insulated themselves, boxing out those who cannot afford it. Derek Thompson, a reporter for the *Atlantic*, writes, "Expensive travel leagues siphon off talented young athletes from well-off families, leaving behind desiccated local leagues with fewer players, fewer involved parents, and fewer resources."[11] Across the country over the past fifteen years, recreational programs have declined by approximately 50 percent. If you do not have the money, you are starting to have no place to play.

The gap has grown, and there is finally a call to Congress to address it. The Commission on the State of US Olympics and Paralympics published their final report in 2024 calling for intervention at the federal level. "Parents have been shortchanged by a pay-to-play system that leaves too many children without access to the health and social benefits of youth sports in their communities," the report says. "Congress has made it clear for decades that Americans' equitable access to sports and fitness in a safe environment is a public value. The time has come for the federal budget to reflect this value."[12]

The recommendation suggests the US Olympic and Paralympic Committee focus on high-performance athletes while Congress "take[s] steps to construct a new architecture for youth and grassroots sports development in our country that serves as both a pipeline for high-performance talent and a pipeline for the better health and other benefits we know sports promote in our communities." The commission calls for Congress to create a new Health and Human Services Office of Sports and Fitness to support the coordination and development of youth and grassroots sports nationwide.[13] Their recommendation includes providing federal grants to level the playing field. Currently it is either nonprofit organizations, like Coalitions for Sport Equity, Project Play, and

Every Kid Sports, that provide funding to address issues of equity, or people have to take the fight to court.

Aligning to create equitable legislation has produced real change. Advocates in New York City created the Fair Play Coalition in 2016 to pursue sports equity for public high schoolers who did not have access to after-school sports programming; "Before the case, 17,000 New York City Black and Latinx public high school students had no PSAL (Public School Athletic League) sports teams whatsoever."[14] They reached a class-action settlement in March 2022 to expand access.

Every underrepresented group needs a vehicle to create equitable access or a champion to put in the energy. It can be fighting in court or proactively building with resources where you are. For example, people like John Anderson, a former college football coach, founded the Castle Rock Incredibles, an organization comprised of special needs athletes in Castle Rock, Colorado. John founded the group when he saw there was not available programming for special needs athletes in the area. He has worked as a coach, mentor, and organizer to keep whom he calls "abilities athletes" playing a sport all year 'round. His energy put equity in action, and thankfully there are many passionate people doing similar work all over the country.

Equity is a challenge because of all the things that make us different: gender, race, ethnicity, ability, and affluence. You want me to really raise the temperature in here? Let's talk about transgender equity. Before we do, I think it's important to separate the equity conversations between elite (college, Olympic, or professional) and youth and high school athletes. My interest is in providing equitable access to the benefit of sports participation we know all kids and teenagers need. Transgender athletes want a fair opportunity to compete, to feel included, and to have a space to use the body that defines them.[15] There are times those with whom they compete (in most instances girls) feel as though it is anything but fair. They feel outmatched and unsafe. Whose feelings of equity matter most? If you answered confidently one of the two groups, then you are not truly interested in equity. If you are willing to entertain the voices of both sides, then there is hope to create peace in the conflict.[16]

Marilou St-Pierre, principal researcher at the University of Laval in Quebec, Canada, was the speaker for a webinar titled "The Inclusion of Trans and Non-Binary People in Sport: It's a Matter for Everyone." They argued, "We need to remember that these are real people with feelings, lives, and families. They want to engage in sport just like everyone else."[17] St-Pierre brought up the argument that sport in and of itself isn't actually fair. The presence of transgender athletes in the youth ranks does not significantly affect the big picture of what sport can provide. Including all athletes or finding a place for them all to play should be the goal.

We create policies and legislation largely in response to emotions. We want to create logical order where emotions dominate. Maybe when we can take out the emotion, there is a way to create a policy that catches equity. Sometimes, the policies we use are too black-and-white when what we need is a fluid shade of gray and a way to make objective, case-by-case decisions.

SPORTS EQUITY TO COMBAT RACISM

Speaking of black and white, there is no way to write a chapter on equity without mentioning race. As my disclaimer, my interviews and the launching of my research started in the communities where we lived and are limited to a handful of participants because I have always lived in predominantly White communities. Those I interviewed about their experiences with racial inequities also live, work, and play in White communities, so their perspectives about race and equity in youth sports are limited to their experiences only.

Pam, a White woman married to a Black man, is the mother of two biracial children, a boy and a girl. Their kids participated in several sports, and they lived in three separate communities: one in Indiana, one in Wisconsin, and the other in Massachusetts. Hockey was the sport the kids were involved with most. "He was the only Black because we lived in very White areas," she said of her son. "There aren't a lot of Blacks in hockey, but I think he would have probably told you, 'There aren't a lot of Blacks in anything I do, period.'" When I sent her a message to ask about details related to an incident in the hockey rink, she asked me, "Which one?"

She wasn't comfortable characterizing regions of the country as less or more racist because their experiences in each community were also influenced by the ages of her kids. When the kids were in elementary school, there had been an incident during a game in Massachusetts. Several other parents had heard a player on the opposing team calling her son the N-word. The men wanted to seek out justice on their behalf by confronting the player and their coach after the game. Pam told me, "I remember being annoyed because I know they were trying to be protective of my son, but they were creating this whole fuss." And she knew her son wouldn't have wanted it to be handled that way.

There were other incidents, too, like one that resulted in a formal complaint sent to the high school referee's association in Indiana. In that instance two Black players on the team, Pam's son and the goalie, were both verbally and physically attacked during a game by an aggressive and mouthy player. After a vicious stick check on the boards, the kid said to Pam's son, "Hey, it's Trayvon Martin. When is he going to get shot again?" And then after spearing the goalie he said, "F–k you, Black lives don't matter." Both moms were part of the filed complaint, and what they were asking for was a way to make the incident an educational one for everyone in the rink. The player involved was ultimately ejected from the game, but there was no announcement of the infraction or acknowledgment of the reason he was dismissed. The two moms whose athletes experienced the racist attack were most disappointed a teachable moment had been missed.

Pam acknowledged that her son experienced less overt instances of racism, and sometimes it came from teammates. Her son would mostly call out the racism when it happened, but there were times he grew tired of the effort. Addressing and fighting racism in the name of justice and equity is a battle we should all be willing to wage. Being mindful of how to do that in a way that honors those most affected is the key. The well-meaning dads who wanted to vehemently defend Pam's son should have asked them what they would have liked to see happen. If an environment is comprised of people too unwilling to change, whether it is parents, coaches, or teammates that create a racially toxic situation, then finding a new place to play might be the only solution. I talk more about handling toxic environments in chapter 9, but one way is to be a positive change agent.

Jeff, a longtime college and high school athletic trainer, is a Black man who lives in a midwestern city that is 93 percent White. He regularly employs a positive-change-agent attitude to diffuse racially charged situations. Not long after he moved to that community, he was attending to a hurt basketball player in a rural gym when a parent came flying out of the stands, yelling, "What are you doing to my kid, boy? Get your hands off him!"

Jeff told me, "I prided myself on staying professional. From my experience, I've changed people's narratives from what they see in an angry Black man to, 'Oh, he's a professional.' You have to figure out which narrative you should believe."

CALL IT OUT
Equity begins with empathy and ends with action. People must be willing to imagine the world from other people's perspectives and then go to bat for those who need help. If you do not have the energy to learn about and support every athlete in your care or sphere of influence with equity and empathy, then you have no business coaching or helping to organize teams of children.

Some youth organizations are changing their cultures by eliminating young-kid tryouts and mandating equal playing time for the athletes who show up to play because that is better for kids. Positive change happened when our school district was called out and held to a legal standard. Positive changes are happening around sports, race, and equity but only because people are willing to have difficult conversations and learn how they can help to make things more fair.

If you are fired up about changes happening in sports, Title IX, race, affluent disparities, transgender athletes, or any other inequity you observe, then how much are you willing to learn about it? Can you see it as a place where growth is possible no matter what you believe now or how it makes you feel? Are you willing to fight to level the playing field? I sincerely hope so.

CHAPTER 8

Sobriety Matters

Drowning Your Feelings Affects the Kids

THE FIFTEEN-YEAR-OLD BOYS KNEW THEY HAD THE RUN OF THE hotel halls. It was almost 11:00 p.m. on a Saturday night of a hockey tournament weekend. The parents had been playing drinking games and cards for hours, and the coach, who was drinking with them, had apparently forgotten about the curfew he had threatened to impose. A small group of the boys decided to tuck into a room to play video games. As they passed by the open bathroom door, a slurred voice called out to them.

"Oh, hey there, boys! Whatcha' doin'?"

The small group stopped midstride, and when they realized a woman stripped from the waist down was peeing, they pushed each other farther into the room with nervous laughter.

I cannot speak to the reasons the parents and coach were drinking so heavily that night, enough that a fully inebriated mother would lose inhibition and call attention to her half-naked self as her son and his teenage buddies walked by. I will say there were plenty of heavily drinking parents and coaches in the club and travel sports scene over the time our kids played. For some sports, like hockey, drinking is an integral part of the experience. Parents would defend their right to enjoy their weekend time commiserating with friends over a few beers, and I don't dispute that. My challenge to all imbibing sports parents and coaches is to consider the why behind their behaviors, make note of the fact that it is far too easy to overindulge, and acknowledge that all choices we make as parents and coaches have a lasting impact on kids.

Very often, the chemicals humans ingest are used for distraction. But distraction from what? Boredom? Sure. To enhance an experience? Often. Sometimes, and too often in youth sports, chemicals, primarily alcohol, are used to squelch negative emotions that bubble. Psychologists call them negative-emotion dampeners. What is your I-want-to-ignore-this-uncomfortable-feeling behavior? We all have one or many ways of avoiding, suppressing, or altering negative emotions. A culturally accepted method people use to distract themselves from the discomfort of feelings like sadness, anger, grief, frustration, and anxiety is to drink alcohol. Dr. Shahram Heshmat explains, "People experiencing aversive psychological symptoms value drinking alcohol, because it helps to alleviate their negative feelings. The drinking removes, at least temporarily, the stress of anxiety."[1]

Sports parents often face anxious feelings surrounding their children's participation in sports. The anxiety can be linked to a number of things, including the interconnectedness of their parent-child relationship and how it ties to a child's performance. They could also have increased anxiety about investment in the activity. Parents with children playing at the highest levels often invest hundreds, sometimes thousands, of dollars into their kids' experiences, as well as intensely sacrifice precious family time. If a child's athleticism is at all tied to hopes of raising a family's status, then those parents can also struggle with how the entire thing feels. It is no wonder that negative or anxious feelings arise when their kid has a bad performance, there are rampant mistakes, the refs are incompetent, or the team loses. Stress and anxiety accompany these negative experiences, and no one wants to feel that way.

Tailgating is a thing for college and professional games, but you can witness that behavior for youth and high school competitions, too. Pregame stops at the pub are "team building" for the parents and a proactive approach to deal with impending difficult emotions. As a coach, I could always tell if there had been a stop at a local watering hole before the parents took their seats in the stands. I could hear them arrive at the stadium from the other side of the field. More and more, pregame prep for parents includes drinking something or lots of somethings with alcohol in it. It can make for a raucous sideline.

Inhibition is impaired when people consume alcohol. According to American Addiction Centers, "through changes in mood and cognition, a person may engage in behaviors they would not consider when sober." It goes on to say, "due to alcohol's ability to disrupt normal brain functioning, it may lead one to be more likely to engage in violent or aggressive behaviors."[2] Now granted, not all people who consume alcohol will become inappropriately inhibited or aggressive, but angry people can become angrier after a few drinks. Not all people will be the *Hoosiers* dad storming onto the basketball court or my dad yelling frustrated comments about the offside rule he never understood, but with any alcohol on board, comments are less controlled, and the potential for undisciplined outbursts increases. Team adult needs to think about how to curb behavior that is starting to be baked into the youth sports culture and is certainly contributing to some of the challenges we all face to provide the most healthful experiences for kids.

It's Being Built into Youth Sports

Alcohol has become such a part of youth sports that it is starting to be a design of the infrastructure. Literally, it is being built into the facilities that are coming online to service youth sports travel and tournaments. Youth associations are securing picnic licenses or alcohol permits to sell alcohol during softball and baseball tournaments. Hockey rinks are being built with rink-side restaurants with viewing tables that can service the parents while their children are practicing or playing. *Forbes* reported on the trend in their 2018 article "The Next Brilliant Idea in Youth Sports Facilities: Entertaining the Parents."[3] Business is expanding around youth sports to include catering to the parents, and in a lot of cases, there has been a movement to use alcohol as the moneymaker. It is more the exception to have sports experiences, and increasingly youth sports experiences, without alcohol.

WHY ARE YOU HAVING A DRINK RIGHT NOW?

It was a warm spring day in Michigan. We were between games of a AAA hockey tournament, and we'd left the confines of the rink to take a walk with our youngest daughter while her sister was inside with her teammates prepping for their next game. I'm not sure who noticed the tailgaters first, but we all noticed when the coach of our older daughter's team pulled up a chair with the parking-lot partiers and extended his own solo cup toward the temporary bartender. He was scheduled to be on the bench in thirty minutes.

What's the big deal, right? It's legal for a legal-aged adult to enjoy a drink or two with other legal-aged adults. What harm could possibly come from a few midday drinks? Likely he was not going to get drunk off a few drinks, but for me, it illuminated the focus of not only the coach but also the parents with whom we found ourselves traveling. It certainly shifted my opinion of this coach that he couldn't refrain until after the day of games was done. It changed my perspective about the families who very readily invited their daughters' coach to drink before he stepped into an instructional role for their kids.

I know the reason the hairs on the back of my neck are raised in instances like this is because I am an educator at my core. I would never consider having a few drinks before stepping into a classroom. This coach and these parents apparently did not see the hockey experience as I did. It was an experience in entertainment for them, and the lessons taught were inconsequential to the people huddled around the cooler.

Admittedly, as the child of an alcoholic, I become immediately sensitive to how and where alcohol exists for the adults involved in youth sports. I was that athlete who would have smelled the alcohol on the breath of a coach coaching me. I would have known he didn't have the discipline to wait until the coaching day was done. Now as a parent, the behavior further confirmed that I was not philosophically aligned with the other adults who were helping to raise our child. We had always wanted youth sports to be educational ground for our kids, and the party part never felt right.

It is a really tough thing to look at our personal relationships with chemicals and how and when we use them and separate our personal choices from the momentum of a group activity that not only involves drinking but also builds it into the fabric of what's happening. Similar to the individuality of a person's sports story, we each carry with us an alcohol story. (And I am going to stick with alcohol because it's the most popular and widely used around sports, but other drugs could easily be part of this conversation, too.) What is your alcohol story? What is your use of alcohol now? When alcohol is tied to athletic experiences, it can affect a person's sport and alcohol stories simultaneously.

I wish I could say I have no alcohol story, but I would be lying. Obviously, I had an interesting upbringing around alcohol, and you would think it would have deterred me from drinking for my entire life, but it didn't. When I think about my alcohol story, I realize how intensely tied to athletics it is. The last game for my college team during my freshman year happened on the road. After the game, the coaches took the graduating seniors out to the bars to celebrate (a.k.a. drown their sorrows for a disappointing season). It must have been a wild night because the van I traveled in that next morning struggled to stay on the road. The assistant coach who was driving was either still drunk or too hungover to drive well. When we stopped for gas, I asked if she would let me drive the team van the rest of the way because she was obviously struggling, and the seniors were not in much better shape. I was eighteen years old, and the fifteen-passenger van was full of my college teammates.

I got behind the wheel and then uncomfortably drove ninety miles an hour to keep up with the head coach, who was in the van ahead of me. Justifiably, one of my passengers relayed her concern about this scenario when she spoke to her mom that evening. (She would have been texting the entire ride, if that was something we did then.) Her mom appropriately called the athletic department to share her dismay. I didn't know at the time that the head coach was already resigning from his position and was not concerned about the riskiness of this episode, and aside from the speed we were driving or the fact that I was behind the wheel of the college-administered van, the end-of-season party was and is normalized behavior for college teams.

What we need to pay attention to is how the observed culture of parent drinking when kids are younger absolutely fuels the behavior in college and beyond. Social drinking and drunkenness are not the same thing, but what kids learn about habitual drinking with sports experiences, especially if the drinking is at all connected to personal or collective anxieties, is that throwing back a few or a lot is completely acceptable and an appropriate method for coping. It sets people up for hazardous drinking behaviors later in life, period. I am fairly certain a majority of people do not even notice the unhealthy level of alcohol saturation that exists in society and as a by-product the machine that is youth sports.

It's not unusual on sidelines, in bleachers, or at postgame team gatherings to hear parents say, "They suck! I need a drink." "I can hardly watch this. I'm going to the bar." "Oh seriously, kid, you're driving me to drink!" Parents within earshot laugh, and then they agree to throw back a few with them either between periods (if you're at the right hockey game), at the bar they visit postgame, or at the hotel pool deck later that night. There is nothing about this behavior that improves the sports experience—for the kids. In fact, studies suggest unhealthy drinking behavior of parents is detrimental to the development of their children: "Adult children of alcoholics (ACOA) had more self-reported stress, more difficulty initiating the use of mediating factors in response to life events, and more symptoms of personal dysfunction than the control group."[4]

"But wait! I'm not an alcoholic!" I can hear you yelling. "I don't drink enough that my kids even notice," you say. If what I have uncovered about alcoholism and what is termed *high-intensity drinking* is accurate, then most parents of youth and high school athletes (especially in Wisconsin, but I know elsewhere) drink much more than they should. If you have regular engagement with alcohol or consistent behavior drinking around sporting events or cannot go an evening without a drink, then you might be drinking too much. It's not hard to drink more than we're supposed to. I was actually surprised by my findings and truly humbled about my own behaviors when expert after expert weighed in about the appropriate amount of alcohol that is safe for adults to consume.

FIVE TYPES OF ALCOHOLICS
There are five categories of alcoholism: young adult alcoholics (the college-aged drinkers who drink the way college kids have been drinking forever), young antisocial alcoholics, functional alcoholics, intermediate familial alcoholics, and chronic severe alcoholics. According to DrugRehab.com, 32 percent of alcoholics in the United States are young adult alcoholics. That category of drinkers on average drink "143 days each year, and they typically consume five or more drinks at a time."[5] Many more people than young adults might recognize their drinking behavior in that description. Drinking has become so normalized and popular that we hardly think about the adverse effects for us personally, much less about how those behaviors are affecting our kids.

Every day of the week can be celebrated with alcohol: "Margarita Monday," "Boozeday Tuesday," "Wednesday Wine or Whiskey Night," "Thirsty Thursday," "Fireball Friday," and then party on the weekends. It is not hard to get to that 143-days-of-drinking mark. You need only drink Fridays, Saturdays, and one more day of each week to hit that threshold. Of course, the amount you drink on those days matters, but I can certainly attest to the ease of multiple-drink consumption each day of a youth sports weekend, especially when the folks I've traveled with for a trip are imbibing, too. It is acceptable and common to achieve binge- or heavy-drinker status on a regular basis. Check out table 8.1. How are you doing?

It has become so normalized to consume more alcohol than is healthy for us that we hardly realize all the damage we are doing to ourselves and to our children. We engage in binge drinking any time we consume more than four or five drinks in a single day. That's way too easy. I am not asserting that every drinking sports parent has an alcohol problem, but I would challenge all parents to take an honest look at their drinking habits, not only as it relates to their involvement with other sporting parents, but also in general.

Table 8.1. Alcohol's Negative Emotional Side

	Binge Drinker	Heavy Drinker
Men 21–64	5+ drinks/occasion	14 or more drinks/week 4 or more drinks on a given day
Women 21+ and Men 65+	4+ drinks/occasion	7 or more drinks/week 3 or more drinks on a given day

Source: Rajita Sinha, "Alcohol's Negative Emotional Side: The Role of Stress Neurobiology in Alcohol Use Disorder," *Alcohol Research: Current Reviews* 42, No. 1 (October 27, 2022), https://arcr.niaaa.nih.gov/volume/42/1/alcohols-negative-emotional-side-role-stress-neurobiology-alcohol-use-disorder.

Why Alcohol Really Has No Place in Youth Sports

Young kids through high-school-aged athletes are watching the adults around them. They absorb drinking behaviors like a dry sponge pulls up spilled drinks. I've watched heavily drinking parents allow and then encourage heavy drinking in their growing teens and most especially after the kids have turned twenty-one. That behavior is cyclical, and kids observe parent behavior from the very start. Kids know if their parents cheer louder at their games after they've gone to the pregame with other parents. They know that the crowd will get rowdier the more alcohol is on board. Everyone knows that. It is normalized, celebrated, and encouraged that alcohol is a fun part of life and especially a fun part of sports. It is also killing us.

According to the National Center for Drug Abuse Statistics, there are 95,000 alcohol-related deaths each year in the United States. More than 47,000 of those deaths are attributed to long-term health failure from drinking.[6] Many of us have drinking habits that challenge our health and well-being and will put our kids on the same track when they become the adults in the room.

Maybe the reason I feel it's important to have the alcohol conversation in a book about youth sports is because those families involved at the highest level of youth sports are the demographic most likely to drink heavily, too. According to a Gallup poll, household income affects the rate of alcohol consumption, with 80 percent of those whose household income is $100,000 or more self-reporting as drinkers. They are also most likely to be involved with highly competitive, travel, and expensive sports. That drinking rate is contrasted by the 49 percent of self-reported drinkers for households with $40,000 or less. The more money you make, the more youth sports opportunities you can buy for your children, and likely the more alcohol will be a part of those experiences.[7]

Young kids and teens need the adults in their world, in their classrooms, on their fields, on their courts, in their rinks, and in their homes to be sober and disciplined more than they are drunk and unruly—that is if we adults value sobriety and discipline in the next generation of humans we are raising. The world has long accepted alcohol as an appropriate drug of choice. We're now tipping the scale for it being a drug of choice that accompanies us as we put our kids in the activities we claim are for their health and well-being. We say sports are supposed to grow our kids through life lessons and offer fertile ground for the character we hope to foster in them. Don't you think they deserve the very best examples around them in the adults they observe?

If you are curious about your drinking habits and whether you should consider your choices, there are a number of self-evaluative online questionnaires that can quickly help you determine if you should take a different course of action with your alcohol use:

- Alcohol Use Disorders Identification Test (AUDIT; https://auditscreen.org/~auditscreen/cmsb/uploads/audit-english-version-new_001.pdf)

- American Addiction Centers' Cutting Down, Annoyance by Criticism, Guilty Feeling, Eye-openers (CAGE) Questionnaire (https://americanaddictioncenters.org/alcohol/rehab-treatment/cage-questionnaire-assessment)

- Michigan Alcohol Screening Test (MAST; https://www.therecoveryvillage.com/alcohol-abuse/mast-alcohol-assessment-quiz/)

Team Chemistry

Choosing Your Personal pH

THERE WAS A LOCKER-ROOM PEEING INCIDENT THAT HAPPENED midseason for one of my son's hockey teams. The team was comprised of eighth- and ninth-grade boys, and there had been several instances of inappropriate adult outbursts and an overt tolerance for what I would term bully behavior by the coach, his staff, and a few of the parents. This latest incident was an indication that I had aligned myself with a culture that was both literally and figuratively toxic—at least for me.

Of the approximately two hundred or so sports communities of which I've been a part, that team ranks among one of the most toxic. Thankfully, I've only been exposed to a couple environments that stand out like that. The common thread in the situations I've endured as an athlete, parent, or coach boils down to tolerated toxic behavior. Either the coach or coaches provided the toxic energy and thus led the group into toxic waters, a big-personality parent or two have changed the chemistry of the group's relationships and thus the environment as a whole, or the toxicity found traction among the athletes because the adults did not do enough to stop its spread. That particular group had the trifecta of unattended toxic behavior at every level, at least from my perspective.

People are not toxic, but their behavior can be. And what's toxic for you may be annoying to me but not necessarily toxic.

What is the definition of toxic behavior? According to WebMD, toxic behavior is "any behavior that adds negativity or upset to your life."[1] Dr. Elizabeth Scott, who writes often about managing stress in the name of improved relationships and emotional well-being, describes a toxic relationship as "one that makes you feel unsupported, misunderstood, demeaned, or attacked. A relationship is toxic when your well-being is threatened in some way—emotionally, psychologically, and even physically."[2]

We do not experience emotional toxicity except as it pertains to our human relationships. Essentially any relationship we have with another person has the potential to be toxic. We know this instinctively. A passionately loving couple can devolve to devastating levels of toxic destruction. Relationships by their very nature are dynamic, and that fluidity is the challenge and the power in human connection. Loretta Graziano Breuning, founder of the Inner Mammal Institute, writes, "We mammals seek the safety of social alliances because that promotes survival. Our social groups have conflict because each brain evolved to focus on its own survival. Mammal groups stick together despite the conflict when they have a common enemy—because that promotes survival. It's not easy being mammal!"[3] When people work on the health of their connections and relationships, they can keep toxic behavior and upset at bay. If there is tolerance for detrimental behavior, then it can quickly spiral out of control, damaging and ultimately destroying relationships and people.

The group of adults who are part of a team don't often think about the chemical composition of their connections. You hear the term *team chemistry* but only so far as it relates to the success of the athletes who get along and perform well together. Team chemistry, especially at the youth and high school levels, depends on the chemistry of the adults, too. As a player, coach, and parent who has been part of so many sports communities, I can attest that there are times chemistry seems to simply happen, but it is also possible to build better chemistry with effort.

Elemental Personalities in Team Chemistry

Each person is comprised of their own combination of elements. Depending on when a person is inserted into a sports community, the chemical makeup they carry can vary. Each person's elements are influenced by their individual sports story, their sports parent or fan personality, the experiences they have, the nature of their relationships with their children playing, how they relate to their spouse or ex-spouse, and how they connect with the other people with whom they've gathered (see figure 9.1 on the following page). You can talk about it as baggage, too, but elements feel more dynamic and better describe the colorful folk who populate sidelines or stands.

At first glance, which personality do you think you are most like? If you were to show it to your spouse, your children, or your friends, who would they say you are most like? These are obviously caricatures, and most people see themselves in several images. I have found using these exaggerated versions of sports parent personalities can launch valuable conversations. The exercise that has been most powerful with this graphic is to show it to high school parents and their athletes at the same time. Before saying anything out loud, they are asked to determine which character best aligns with the parents' personality in and around their children's sports. It is not uncommon that the athlete and the parents have different perspectives about which generalized characters are most like their parents. It starts an interesting conversation.

Then, I have asked the parents and athletes which of the personalities is most toxic to them. In a room full of athletes, the most popular response has been Yelling Yolanda. Groups of parents will most often choose Car Coach Carl, Expert Eddie, or Yelling Yolanda. Coaches have landed on Gossiping Georgina, Expert Eddie, and Delusional Dan as most toxic to them, while

Analyzing Allen	Bean-Counting Bernie	Bribing Bobby	Broadcaster Brett	Cameraman Chris
Car Coach Carl	Clueless Carrie	Crafting Cathy	Dead-Serious Doug	Delusional Dan
Enthusiastic Eugene	Expert Eddie	Fearful Freddie	Gossiping Georgina	Hands-Off Harry
Manipulator Mack	Meal-Planning Mary	Money Mike	Negative Nancy	Nervous Nelly
No-Work-No-Way Noah	Party Pete	Playing Polly	Rule-Reader Randy	Safety Sharon
Super-Fan Stan	Volunteer Vera	Whistle-Blowing-Wendy	Win-at-All-Cost Wilma	Yelling Yolanda

Figure 9.1. Sports Parent Personalities

groups of administrators have felt more inclined to point to Manipulator Mack as the most toxic. These opinions often happen before I provide a more robust description of each personality. It seems most people have a pretty clear sense of these colorful and minimized versions because our shallow impressions of the other people in the stands around us is enough to recognize these hyperbolized characters.

When I have time for the longer version of this exercise, I provide lengthier descriptions of each character, and then I challenge people to think about the good and bad potential for each personality. There are certainly positive ways to use default sports parent personalities. Take, for example, my friend Janel. When I met Janel, she was incredibly busy as the sports mother of three athletes in various stages of competition. Her oldest was playing high school and club basketball, her middle son was playing club basketball and soccer on middle-school-aged teams, and her daughter was just signing up for her first teams as an elementary-aged player. Janel is a passionate parent and fan. You notice her. She cheers, she moves, and she is always incredibly engaged. It is an energy that has led to the occasional conflict with the coaches of her kids.

I was already coaching the boys high school team when Janel's middle son entered the program as a freshman. I had presupposed correctly that she was going to bring passion to our program. I knew she was passionately engaged in our games, sort of like Playing Polly, and we were able to put her to work occasionally as a ball person. It gave her a purposeful focus and a reason to continue moving while the boys were playing. Instead of squelching her energy, she and I worked together to find ways for her to put it to use. She began to employ similar positive participation for other teams for which her kids played. Part of the transformation I saw in her over the years was because she became a seasoned sports parent, but the other reason was because she purposefully pursued growing through her experiences and used her energy in the most positive ways she could.

Creating conversation and then empowering the players to engage their parents with a shared language had a generally positive effect, too. During one of our team personality checks, a player shared that he thought his dad was part Yelling Yolanda and part Expert Eddie. The dad hadn't identified himself that way, instead thinking he was an Analyzing Allen, but he remained open to his son's perspective. At a game later that season, the dad was caught on film yelling expert instruction, and his son looked directly at him and raised a shushing finger to his lips. The dad got the message and was quiet the rest of the game. Creating space for that conversation affected progress in the relationship for both of them.

PERSONAL CHEMISTRY: ELEMENTS THAT AFFECT US

Both positive and negative hormones influence our engagement as fans at a sporting event. Hormones are the neurotransmitters in our brains that essentially build the emotional stories of our experiences, and "atypical levels of neurotransmitters in the brain can affect emotions."[4] When our brains are flooded with hormones, we have an emotional experience.

What chemical messages do our brains send while we're on the sidelines, and how do those messages influence the emotions we must navigate there? The hormones that trigger positive emotions in our brains are dopamine, serotonin, endorphin, and oxytocin, "happy brain chemicals," according to Breuning.[5] Dr. Richard Shuster, clinical psychologist and host of the *Daily Helping* podcast, claims that "when your team [and I would say your child, too] wins or is playing well, your brain starts releasing the neurotransmitter dopamine, which is directly involved in regulating the brain's reward and pleasure centers."[6]

Negative emotions are most often blamed on cortisol, the hormone connected to stress. Adrenaline is the culprit that carries all the chemicals through our bodies with crazy speed. Watching a team or child who is struggling, disappointing, or frustrating has potential to increase the stress hormone cortisol, and circumstances in the game can fire the adrenaline response. When you become angry at a bad call, at a vicious foul, or at a comment from people around you, adrenaline and cortisol surge in your body. Jason Whiting explains,

> The amygdala is an almond-shaped piece of your brain attuned to threats and emotional responses [like those that ride adrenaline and cortisol waves]. When the amygdala lights up, the prefrontal cortex—where we do our logical thinking and reflecting—is bypassed, and our emotional brain goes on high alert. A shout from the amygdala causes a lot of feelings but very little thinking.[7]

Your heart rate goes up, and you start to lose the ability to have rational thought. Depending on your awareness of this surge in hormones and thus emotion and your ability to quickly process it, you may struggle to think clearly and behave in undesirable ways. The Mental Health Foundation states, "When anger gets in the way of rational thinking we may give way to the urge to act aggressively, propelled by the instinct to survive or protect someone from a threat."[8] That freak-out moment of the crazy parent seems out of control because it is.

The hockey fight I broke up when our son was nine happened because I was tightly packed between two passionately yelling dads. They were losing the ability to think rationally, and my silence was not an option; I chose to out-yell them, using positive encouragement only. It confused them enough to stop the hormone surge that could have led to a more physical altercation. The release of hormones is a common human process, but learning what to do about those naturally occurring processes changes the way we show up. We need to stabilize the chemical composition of our bodies to give us the best shot to increase positive hormones and reduce the hormones that don't serve us or our children.

It's a known mantra: Nutrition, sleep, and exercise lead to a healthful life. They are the key to creating the right balance of chemicals for happier brains and emotional stability, too.

Obviously, the chemicals we ingest in our food and drink literally become chemicals in our bodies. Sugar is the bad-mood food for a reason. It jacks with the hormones insulin and serotonin. Caffeine is tricky. It increases levels of cortisol and decreases serotonin levels, but it also may increase dopamine and oxytocin levels.[9] Alcohol initially releases the feel-good hormones of dopamine, serotonin, and oxytocin, but chronic or binge consumption of alcohol "can alter a person's natural production of these 'feel good' hormones. Levels of cortisol . . . also rise with increased alcohol consumption, and with alcohol withdrawal."[10] We are what we eat, and we feel what we eat.

Sleep, or lack thereof, profoundly affects hormone health. One study found that the "release of hormones by the pituitary—the 'master' endocrine organ that controls the secretion of other hormones . . . is markedly influenced by sleep."[11] The findings concluded that all body systems were affected by sleep deprivation, completely disrupting optimal hormonal function. Cortisol appears frequently in tandem with chronic stress and fatigue. Creating a healthy sleep habit will chemically change your body.

Endorphin is the other controllable happy hormone and is released when we exercise. I know many youth sports arenas are outfitting themselves with bars so parents and fans can imbibe, attracting them to the very real happy hormones that initially come with alcohol, but maybe the better decision would be to put treadmills and stair masters in those spaces instead. That way parents can increase their own endorphin levels while watching their kids play. Knowing that likely won't happen, you can still make the decision to move when your kids do. Walk while they are practicing, run while they are warming up, or seek out a local aerobics class to attend between tournament games. You will feel better, and your hormones and probably your children will thank you.

Oh yeah, there is one more thing you can do to enhance your happy hormones and lessen that ugly cortisol one: Pray or meditate. I joked with a few hockey moms once that I was going to start a yoga class in the lobby so we could all center ourselves and regain control of our perspectives. I wasn't wrong to believe that activity would balance hormones and emotions. Deep meditation and prayer are linked with plenty of health and hormonal benefits. They increase serotonin and endorphins and reduce levels of cortisol.[12] As long as you don't expect your deep breathing or purposeful prayer to alter the outcome of the game, you will find benefit in the exercise.

CHEMICAL BONDS AND REACTIONS

OK, so let's assume you've done all the personal work you needed to get your chemical composition to its absolute healthiest level. You roll up your little yoga mat, sip on your power shake, and slide into the stands at your child's game. Likely you are one of only a handful, if that, who has shown up that way to take in the day's game. You find yourself sitting alongside all the various chemical vessels in the coaches, parents, and grandparents around you. It's hard to know if the chemicals that have come together that day are going to be a powder keg or a delectable recipe. What can be done when the enlightened version of yourself must engage with those other chemical compounds over which you have no control? What control can we assert?

We have three choices about how to engage with others in our youth sports environments. We can wither, shrinking away from and avoiding the energies that do not align with ours. We can withstand and let our energy fold into the mix of characters. Or we can become a change agent and do something on purpose to affect the chemistry around us. I admit I have employed all three strategies at one point or another.

I interviewed my sister Catherine, the D-I all-American soccer player, about how the Yelling Yolandas make her feel as a parent. Catherine said, "It bothers me to the point I can't sit next to some parents because of how they yell at their kids. It's not so much that they are yelling at other kids; it's at their kids and it's not helping them. It just makes it worse." At the time of our interview, her twin daughter and son were twelve years old, and she was navigating the preteen nuttiness, a time fraught with emotion for adults and kids. She was employing the wither strategy on the soccer sidelines for her daughter (a regular strategy of mine when I am on the fan side of soccer games, too). She and I both remember never noticing the yelling of parents or coaches while we played but being incredibly sensitive to it as parents.

The withstanders are just that: those who stand with and engage in the behaviors of those around them. It's the fan experience enjoyed as a collective, and when the energy is good, it's a great place to be. It is possible for that group energy to shift quickly, however, and swallow up anyone who is a part. I talk more about mob mentality and groupthink in the next chapter.

And then there are the change agents. Those folks are like the catalyst in a chemical reaction: a substance that lowers the activation energy of a reaction or speeds it up without being consumed by the reaction.[13] A catalyst can influence its environment by either stirring the pot into action or providing the stabilizing force to calm things down. Pot-stirring catalysts come in all forms in youth sports. They are the Enthusiastic Eugenes and Super-fan Stans who motivate a crowd to cheer and get engaged, and they can also be the Gossiping Georginas who spread catalyzing words in all sorts of ways. They make action happen, and the action can be either good or bad.

The stabilizing catalysts for group-engaged emotional events are rarer than the pot stirrers and are generally people with great emotional discipline. In the high school world, those people need to be activities and athletic directors or the administrators in charge of events. For the youth teams not associated with schools, there is a problem with consistent and effective stabilizers. Tournament directors need to be prepared to play that role, and it is valuable if teams identify and possibly even assign people to that job if too many emotionally charged incidents surround the team.

Seasoned parents with some "immunity" are a good choice. They are the folks who seem immune to toxicity. Either they are incredibly emotionally disciplined, or by being exposed to toxic incidents, they've built up tolerance. They are often the ones armed to step in and suggest changes to bad behavior, even in the moment.

The hardest year I experienced coaching high school soccer happened without much administrative support at all. A number of emotionally charged instances plagued the team, and I was without a stabilizing force in an administrator or a fan/parent on the sideline who could calm things down. Knowing the next season was going to be similarly unsupported, I assigned the most emotionally stable parent I knew to the job of fan patrol/shusher. Knowing that that was his role changed the energy on the fan sidelines not only for him but also for all the parents who knew he had been given that job.

There are a few things to note about how and when to employ stabilizing strategies. I tried to stand up in protection of the boys on my son's squirt hockey team once. I learned the hard way that calling a full parent meeting to discuss undesirable behavior of the parent coaches without talking to them first is not actually all that stabilizing. It became the ignition to dynamite instead. Unsolicited advice for stabilization is generally difficult to deliver and often ill received. If you are witness to or in any way part of a toxic interaction, employing the role of catalyst can lower the temperature in the room and change the destructive reaction brewing, but approach matters.

I interviewed Alicia twice, once in 2012 and then again by email in 2019. She was an incredible athlete in her own right. She has had leadership roles as an athletic director, business owner, and coach, as well as the job of mom to two high-level athletes. During the seven years between interviews, Alicia was quite active in learning and proactively engaging herself in the youth sports world. She shared a story with me in our second interview that highlights the challenges and necessary influence of catalysts.

Her high school daughter told her about an upsetting experience with her teammates and coach. They had lost a game, and one teammate began to cry. She wrote, "In so many words [the coach] told her to get over it. Then started in on the team and how bad they played and telling them they should feel disappointed with their play." The girls had mixed responses to the coach's berating, and one girl protected the crier, and the other protected the coach. She continued,

> The coach heard those two girls and yelled at them that they were dividing the team, then started asking players as they were leaving the locker room which side they were on. He then proceeded to call those two back in with another coach and started lecturing the first girl about how she needed to care more about the loss. She asked to leave the situation, but they wouldn't let her—a very unsafe environment for that girl to be in.

The situation expanded to conversations among the dads, and Alicia struggled with how to step in when she was not personally connected to either girl, but she was intent on stabilizing what had certainly become a toxic environment for at least several of the girls (and thus their parents). Alicia waited for a good time to speak with the coach directly and privately about her concerns. She assured the mother of the more vulnerable player that her emotions were valid and offered her support as they navigated the situation. She also addressed the incident with her daughter to come alongside her as she navigated, too. They were still processing the emotion of the incident, but Alicia had handled it as a seasoned and well-equipped catalyst should.

Alicia could have withered, or she could have withstood and joined in the gossip, but instead she chose to be a change agent. There is no surefire way to attend to all the chemical imbalances that happen within a group of people, but knowing we have a choice in how we engage should empower all of us.

Master Chemist

A well-equipped and seasoned leader who has the capacity and willingness to tinker with the pH of the entire group usually does it best before a season starts and then maintains that consistency throughout. One youth hockey season, I prayed for our son to be cut from the A team because I wanted him to play for a coach I had come to admire. Coach Jay did all the right things to set the tone for a positive-growth environment and a stabilized adult group. He invested his energy into efforts of team and relationship building for both the players and the parents. His investment in those relationships has allowed him to continue his positive connection with parents from that team as they blossomed into lifelong friendships. It was the sort of effort that built team chemistry that might not have otherwise been there. We should celebrate and become the Coach Jays of the world, building healthful and positive community for everyone involved.

Being a part of teams and families is a dynamic endeavor. It is not static because it is a people job that continually responds to the elements who show up, the experiences we have individually and as a group, and the decisions each person makes about their engagement in the process.

CHAPTER 10

Be the Best I in Team

Intentional about Teamwork

THE BAR THE PARENTS CHOSE FOR THE WE-NEED-TO-TALK-about-the-coach meeting was centrally located, about twenty minutes from each community. High school girls' hockey teams in Wisconsin are often co-op arrangements. This particular co-op team was comprised of 80 percent of the girls from one community, while the other schools, our home district included, provided the other 20 percent of the team. The nature of rival schools having to come together to provide a team opportunity for hockey-playing girls makes for an interesting dynamic.

Our daughter was a junior goaltender for the team, and we had watched marked program advancement over the three years she played. My husband helped often as the goalie coach. The young team still struggled to compete with other conference opponents, but they were improving every year. Some of the parents that year, comprised mostly of the younger players, were not happy, so they called a meeting to talk about what could be done about the coach.

The meeting room door closed, and several parents seated themselves around the table, some with beer in hand. The grievances were many and included frustration with line assignments, power play design, practice plans, and losing games they shouldn't have. There was not a single concern about abuse, intolerance, berating, or cruelty. Everything that upset the parents had to do with wins and losses and falling short of their expectations for the season. At first I listened quietly, hoping to understand the impetus behind the energy. As the conversation increased in intensity, I began to suggest including the girls' voices and opinions, wondering if the parents were voicing their own concerns or if the concerns belonged to their daughters, as well. There were no administrators from any of the high schools in attendance, although it was an invitation that had been extended to them. Through the course of the evening, I felt less and less comfortable with where the conversation was headed, and I was increasingly frustrated that a meeting like this could happen without the attendance of the coach in question or an administrator.

It was a situation rife with emotion, and there was not enough objectivity in the room. I found myself defending the coach, pushing to get input from the girls, and encouraging them to more formally include administrators in any additional conversation. We left the meeting with that plan.

Appropriately, the lead athletic director put a stop to the parent-led coup. He declared that he would conduct a department-designed postseason survey for the players to complete. I was relieved he had reclaimed control. Of the things administrators worry about at the high school level, there was not enough negative student opinion to warrant any sort of discipline for the coach, and there were definitely no grounds for dismissal. The coach was provided the feedback, and he continued to coach and improve on what his administrator suggested. Two and a half years later, that coach took that same team of players (now mostly seniors) to the state tournament. They won the state championship. The administrator did his job to keep parents in the parent lane and supported the coach to improve in his coaching lane. It's unfortunate the lines got so blurry in the first place.

When I began my research, I asked the respondents of my survey what the goal of youth sports should be. They were asked to select as many options as they wanted, and the number 1 choice, with more than 91 percent of the respondents choosing it, indicated that a goal of youth sports should be "to teach kids how to be part of a team." Yet simultaneously, those same respondents admitted to a different focus when it came to the choices parents made through their behaviors. Interestingly, more than 85 percent of the respondents "believed parents of athletes were more interested in individual achievement above team success," and when pushed further about decisions parents made for their child, 95 percent of the respondents said "parents make most of their decisions to better their child above bettering the team." That is in stark contrast to what they believed about the athletes. Forty-six percent believed athletes made their decisions "for the success of the team." The survey revealed a disconnect between what the adults say should be the goal (teaching kids to be part of a team) and the behaviors they employ to achieve it (only thinking about their own children).

As we work to improve our "team" behavior, it is important to note the various team experiences possible as children journey through youth sports. Each type of team requires nuanced understanding of how roles work in each environment. Recreational teams are usually volunteer run and require cooperative efforts among all adults. Parents are often coaches, managers, and board members, and it takes everyone to keep things running. Competitive teams may have a similar structure, depending on the size of the community or the sports association. Look for groups that have a good leadership board, bylaws for their organization, and clearly defined roles of administration and parents. Travel and elite teams can be part of larger systems, or they can operate independently. Coaches are generally paid, and the board may or may not be comprised of parents associated with the team. Solid board structure with a clearly outlined mission statement and bylaws will help take confusion and frustration out of the mix for parents. School teams, at least at the high school level, have well-established structures of administration that create stability within a school, a conference, and the state level. Breakdowns are still possible, as I explain later in this chapter.

No matter what, all youth teams are part of a larger team system. If we want children and teens to learn how to be part of a team, then we adults need to model how that is done and become better teammates ourselves. Our decisions to support the team need to be overt and observable.

It is an approach of parenting that is in line with some of the positive psychology I cover in the final chapter. Educational psychologist Heather Lonczak explains, "In a nutshell, positive parents support a child's healthy growth and inner spirit by being loving, supportive, firm, consistent, and involved. Such parents go beyond communicating their expectations, but practice what they preach by being positive role models for their children to emulate."[1] In the team setting, that would include becoming a role model for how to be part of a team. It is not enough to simply say we think it's important. Secret parent meetings that disrupt team cohesion are exactly the opposite of modeling good teamwork.

We, the collective adult team in youth sports, should make decisions with our child's interests first, which would include being helpful to the teams they are on. There are times, however, if we align with the wrong people, a collective idea may or may not be the best decision for the team. Sometimes sports parents hear others in the stands near them say, "Something should be done," about whatever it is that is making them uncomfortable. There is agreement in that thought, and then the group can quickly create a common enemy. The alignment feels better than sitting alone with bad emotions, so a plan is pursued.

We are wired to belong to social groups, and when the group with which we align suffers from negative experiences collectively, like a disappointing, losing season, it is a rather normal human decision to sidle up beside those who also echo our frustrations and confirm our inclinations to course correct—even if the course correction is not our job.

What is accomplished when parents go behind closed doors or crowd around a table in a bar to dissect and decide the direction of a team *without the players and without the coach or coaches*? It's an echo chamber that, without a doubt, can have an effect. More and more, parent pressure has changed dynamics of teams and programs because of what is likely related to groupthink.

Social psychologist Irving Janis first proposed the theory of groupthink in 1972. He applied his thoughts to policy decisions, but other researchers have noted elements of the theory present in much less consequential decision making that happens in groups. Essentially, groupthink is a "mode of thinking in which individual members of small cohesive groups tend to accept a viewpoint or conclusion that represents a perceived group consensus, whether or not the group members believe it to be valid, correct, or optimal."[2]

Humans have very little patience. When you add time constraints, like the length of a season or a four-year stint in a high school program, and things aren't going well, we feel like we need to do something about it right now. We look for ways to feel in control of a situation that is truly out of our control. Choosing a scapegoat happens much more often than it should because we do not like waiting out or processing uncomfortable situations. As described in a chapter about group psychology written by social psychologist Diana Sanchez, awareness of symptoms that can lead to groupthink "include overestimating the group's skills and wisdom."[3] Parents certainly have expertise about their own children but often assume they know more about what happens within a team than they actually do. They listen to their children wrestle challenging emotions related to their participation and feel compelled to do something about it. Often they form their opinions without all the necessary information, or they follow their compulsion to address their own uncomfortable feelings.

The meeting at the bar did not include the most consequential voices for the conversation. It worked only to assure the frustrated parents that they were not alone in wanting things to change. Seeking that personal assurance was a natural approach, but it was detrimental to the efforts of the team as a whole. As the group moved forward with intention to push the coach out, it was probable that some of the members of the cohesive group did not want to be left out. Sanchez writes,

> When researchers used a functional magnetic resonance imaging scanner to track neural responses to exclusion, they found that people who were left out of a group activity displayed heightened cortical activity in two specific areas of the brain. . . . These areas of the brain are associated with the experience of physical pain sensations. It hurts, quite literally, to be left out of a group.[4]

The human default when those we care about are moving toward a group consensus is to align with them.

In the case of the bar meeting, it was helpful that I was already an outsider to the cohesive unit of parents. I was not from their community, I was not in their friend group, and voicing the perspective of a coach was dissent enough to challenge the groupthink. And then thankfully the administrator did the right thing to put out the fire. It doesn't always go that way, though.

One quick Google search yields story after story of coaches choosing to step down in the midst of parent pressure to do so. As I interviewed people, I heard stories of a lacrosse coach in Colorado, a baseball coach in Minnesota, and a soccer coach in California who could not withstand the parent attacks they faced and thus ended their time coaching. A 2016 article posted on TwinCities.com lists about a dozen instances of high school coaches suffering at the hands of disgruntled parents. One such coach had been one I knew from our time living in Minnesota.[5]

The successful girls high school hockey coach from Stillwater had resigned amid verbal attacks against his family. He was an incredibly successful coach for whom I had developed a high level of respect. In his letter of resignation to district administrators, which was released to various media publications, he wrote,

> Recently, I have seen my family being subjected to an unrelenting and vicious personal series of verbal attacks from a group of parents of intensity unlike any I could have imagined, much less seen before. Much of the joy in coaching in this program has been taken away by the need to defend my own family from these vicious attacks, which would seem to be channeled to and through your office. In the past, I might have shrugged much of this off, confident that I could move forward with the program and an administration that "had my back." I simply will not put my family through any more of this.[6]

His family he wrote about included two of his high school–aged daughters who had been rostered on the team that year.

Other public comments about the situation confirmed the groupthink aspect of this story. In a statement released by the Girls Hockey Booster Club Board members, they explained they were "dismayed by the actions of a small minority of former and current families." They went on to say, "The actions of a disgruntled few are not reflective of the wide majority of current families associated with our program."[7]

Having coached for fourteen years, the coach endured his first losing season, and the most vicious and ultimately defining attacks leveled against him happened while he was coaching his own daughters. He was failed by administration while enduring his most intense years as a coach and parent. I don't know the details of how he managed things while his girls were on the roster, but he'd coached long enough to have the tools he needed to adjust to what might have gone awry. He was not given time to do that because his support system failed. People created motion before attending to the reasons they felt compelled to move.

How were those parents fielding all the ugly and hard emotions that walked in the door with their children? Or if it was not their child's emotions to which they were attending, then did they do anything to acknowledge or mitigate their own feelings? When parents find allies in their struggle, it's just the environment they need to get groupthink wheels rolling. Aligning with others to do something about difficult emotions gives everyone the justification to act on their own feelings of disgust or discomfort. Sometimes that energy is directed at other players or other families, but I would say, more often than not, coaches take the blame and the vitriol. No one is immune to upset opinions of others. In the right circumstances and with the emotionally energized attack of even a few parents, team integrity and a coach's position within that team can be severely damaged or destroyed.

I, too, was attacked. One season we were really successful, and the next season, under different circumstances with a few changes to personnel, injuries, and struggling team leadership, we were anything but successful. I was on the long bus ride home with the team after a game we tied but could have won, while a small group of parents stopped for dinner on their way back. Their meeting was not as formal as the hockey one I had attended as a parent, but it was also at a bar and included a small group of passionate, disappointed, and frustrated parents. The email that was crafted after that meeting went initially to the athletic director, who mistakenly told them to forward it on to me. Every part of the conflict chain of communication we laid out for our program had been ignored: Athletes talk to the coach first. Athletes who feel things are not resolved can invite parents in for a conversation with the coach, and if it still cannot be resolved, then a meeting would be scheduled with the athlete, the parents, the coach, and an administrator. All such meetings need to happen in person.

Had protocol been followed, what felt like an attack would never have happened. The parent who wrote the email expressed that his athlete had spoken to me. They hadn't. There was never an invitation to meet in person with the athlete or the parents. The initial email went directly to the administrator, who, instead of encouraging the parent to forward it on, should have followed through with all of it and kept it from landing in my inbox in the first place. The general sentiment of so many of the good coaches who cannot withstand attacks on what they are doing is that they do not feel supported. In those instances, and as it turned out for me, there wasn't a dissenter in the groupthink gathering, and there wasn't administrative support when there should have been.

Teams can fail us. They can effectively devour us if we are on the wrong side of a collective decision. Most upset in and around teams starts with dysfunctional relationships and more often than not can be traced back to poor communication. It is in those moments we must slow down and remember what role we're being asked to play on any given team. If you're the coach, then coach and recognize your capacity to develop and maintain a culture with what you tolerate. If you're the parent, then parent. Yes, that means making decisions that are important to your own child, but if you have chosen to help support their involvement in a team activity, then at least some of your behavior should be in obvious support of what the team is trying to do. If you are a parent/coach, then know you are straddling a jagged fence with hot lava on either side. Choose team needs every time. Everyone should try to take out the emotion that comes with performance and reflect about whether our behaviors are those of a good team-mate or those of someone who works to break apart the team from the inside.

Administrators and coaches are an important part of the teams they manage. They have the integral job of making solid, objective decisions void of emotion for all parties involved. It is not the parent's job to figure out a way to win. It is not the coach's job to tell the parents how to raise their children, and keeping those boundaries is extremely important. That means the coach who gossips about players with his managers, other players, or parents tears at the fabric of a team. It's a subtle behavior that challenges the building of trust. A gossiping coach willing to gossip about anyone is trusted by no one. It creates a culture that tolerates secret meetings all over the place.

Secrecy is destructive to teams and can be dangerous, too. I interviewed twin sisters whose coach had not crossed the line completely but who had certainly misused his position as a youth softball coach. He became the girls' coach when they were twelve. Very soon after beginning his work with the team, he began to take on the role of a father for this pair of girls. Their mom was a single mom, and Dad was not in the picture. Kristy and Natalie both got some preferential treatment from the coach. He would buy them clothes and equipment and treat them to lunch every once in a while. He did seem to give more attention to Kristy, and things started to get really weird about the time the girls turned sixteen.

Natalie told me,

Yeah, there was this one trip we took for preseason training. Our coach refused to come out of his room to come to practice. I went in to talk with him and asked him why he wouldn't coach. He was distraught and said, "Kristy's not talking to me." I remember saying something like, "She's sixteen, and you're the coach, and what are you talking about? The whole team needs this practice." He eventually did go to practice, but it was weird.

I asked Kristy what she found strange about the coach's affection for her. She said,

He would give me the kind of stuff that I could use, and it was actually stylish, as opposed to the older clothes we had, you know. I didn't mind that he would give us that stuff. I kind of freaked out when he wanted me to see his house before he moved in to make sure that I approved of that. I remember that being really weird. I had to go look at the house after he moved in, too, and I remember going in and seeing like a wall shrine of all these pictures of me. Like that kind of freaked me out, too. I think as I got older, I was old enough to understand a little bit more, and that was definitely creepy.

I asked them how this relationship with their coach affected the team dynamic. Kristy said, "I wonder how much people disliked it or if they could see the favoring that he gave me, if that affected them at all."

"Did you see that?" I asked.

"No, I just wonder, did people talk about it behind my back?"

Natalie chimed in, "I didn't hear anything, but they wouldn't have talked about it around me anyway." Girls are observant, and it is hard to imagine a dynamic such as this would go unnoticed by a team full of teenage girls, much less their parents.

I asked the girls where their mom was in all of this, recognizing that the coach had overstepped his role and assumed a very dysfunctional relationship that could have morphed into something much worse than it did.

"Our mom thought everything was fine," Natalie said.

Kristy agreed, "Yeah, she had him to our house for dinners and everything. She didn't notice the creepy stuff."

Whether the coach was intending to do anything untoward with Kristy or any of the other players on the team who might have received similar treatment, he was employing several strategies of grooming. Tactics of grooming he used included "going above and beyond to be overly helpful to a child or family, showing special attention or interest in a child or vulnerable adult, giving gifts to a child or their family, and attempting to have regular one-on-one time with a child."[8]

Other instances of youth coach missteps that were shared with me or that I observed happened with young coaches just out of high school or college. Drawing the line of relationship with athletes, who are essentially their peers, is a challenge for young coaches. They must be incredibly sensitive to the lines established and to never consider romantic or inappropriate pursuit of the athletes who are on teams for whom they are in charge.

Emotional abuse, physical abuse, or any behavior that is an abuse of a coach's position as a trusted leader can destroy not only the team but also athletes on those teams. No matter how good the team is, how important a spot on that team is, or what you believe being a part of a team with coaching like that can do for your sports career, toleration of abusive behavior only lets it persist and never ends well.

If we are going to do team well, when a group of adults comes together in the name of facilitating or organizing youth or high school athletes into the team environment, it is important to be in pretty close agreement about what that means. A team is a "number of persons forming one of the sides in a game or contest." A team is also described as a "number of persons associated in some joint action."[9] The adults who come alongside youth athletes to provide sports programming are part of that second sort of team. There are a few characteristics of parents and coaches that help to create a picture of how we should try to show up in whatever role we have. Choosing to be intentional about the role you have each season is a choice that can change the outcome for everyone.

I presented nine different characteristics of a good team parent for my survey. Respondents were instructed to "choose the *three* best words or phrases to describe a good team parent." The number 1 vote getter, at more than 83 percent, was to be positive. The close second, at nearly 80 percent, was to "encourage all players." And the third vote getter, at just about 57 percent, described a good sports parent as someone who "supports the coach." The two characteristics that barely received any votes at all (no more than

1 percent) to describe a good team parent was "vocal" or someone who "challenges the coach."

Respondents were asked to "choose the three best words or phrases [out of fifteen options] to describe a good team coach." The top two characteristics chosen, receiving 57 percent and 56 percent, respectively, were "positive" and "teacher." I did not tease out the ages of the kids being coached, and that might have influenced responses, but I think a positive teacher describes the sort of coach we would want for any type of team.

Some teams are more education focused, and some teams rely heavily on entertainment value (win focused, flashy travel experiences, and swag). No matter what, all teams teach something, and it's important to be mindful of the lessons available in any team's offering. If you have chosen to enroll your family in sports that market the entertainment you'll enjoy, then you and your children may be surrounded by adults and kids who are also there for the entertainment. A lot more drama can happen if those involved do not enjoy the show.

As your children journey through their sports, you can only control your own work in that story. What sort of teammate are you choosing to be? Maybe you'll consider this acronym as a pocket guide:

Teachable spirit: Have one. Be willing to learn about your kids, their teammates, the others on the sideline, and the coach in charge. Most of all, seek to learn more about how you can do your role well.

Expect varying expectations, then manage them. No two people expect the exact same things out of an experience. Put in the work to identify your own expectations, and recognize what control you actually have to affect them. Also, do what you can to determine if your expectations are realistic.

Ask curious questions of your athletes. Think about whether the question is leading to what you want them to say or if it is neutral. You can keep in the back of your mind the answer you think they might give, but listen to the answer they actually do give.

Motivate the athletes to go after their own goals. It is not your job to create, modify, or pursue their goals for them, but you truly can serve them by motivating and supporting them to put in the hard work to go after their goals themselves.

No matter what adult role you have on a team, be the best *I* in team you can: **I**ntentional about all of it.

CHAPTER II

Good Grief

Cuts, Losses, Injuries, and Endings

My dad died in October 2022, when I was about halfway done writing the first draft of this book. Much of the pain I've endured in my life, both in and out of sports, points back to my complicated relationship with him and the grief that exists because of how we lost him.

I'm not sure when I started to grieve, but I began writing about it in journals dating back to fifth grade. It was about the same time he moved out of our house, and I realized he was not coming back. I have been processing grief for close to forty years. That's what those early childhood traumas can do. They can rip us open early, gut us, and we will slowly bleed out if we don't do anything about it. For a lot of people, they stuff these wounds with any gauze or distraction they can find to stop the bleeding and protect that vulnerable place. Emotional walls are built.

Grief work is so, so hard. Because of that, I contend that a pretty high percentage of people carry some level of grief that they have no intention of working through. To touch it is to poke at the pain, and if it is buried deep enough, digging down to it is pretty painful, too. In the sporting context, there are both minor and major grief experiences. If someone carries other personal grief from outside the sporting arena, then there are experiences that approach and occasionally break open what they have worked hard to guard. It is possible to hit a grief nerve that evokes an intense emotional response.

I heard a really good definition of grief that counselor Kate Greenway shared in a program on Wisconsin Public Radio:

> Grief is a normal and natural reaction stemming from a loss of any kind. Grief can encompass physical sensations; a wide range of thoughts; provocative spiritual questions; and many, many complex feelings, such as intense sadness, numbness, anger, relief, guilt, despair, hostility, and anxiety. There is no timetable or recipe, no right way to grieve. Each experience of grief is unique.[1]

Sports offer a way to process emotions we don't really want to touch but we know are there. Grief is one of those untouchables. The extreme emotions of the sports experience are grief and elation, but people really only want to experience the latter. It is imperative, however, to acknowledge the ways grief shows up in the youth sports context, so we can all work through it and provide the kids who are growing there the stitches and healing balm to move to a better place.

Grief is described as a deep sorrow. Youth sports grief is a sorrow connected to loss or ending and can best be described as a "mourning of expectations."[2] The greater the expectation, the deeper that sports grief can cut. High-level investment that doesn't pan out or losing a hard-fought important game can bring athletes, fans, parents, and coaches to sorrowful tears. That same emotion appears when an athlete is relegated to the training room or sidelines because of an injury and cannot play, when an athlete doesn't make the cut, or when a sports dream ends. Identifying the presence of grief is the first step to properly addressing its effect on both athletes and the members of team adult who may be expected to journey with them through the tough stuff. For the accompanying adult, if they harbor feelings of grief themselves, then it can be one of the most difficult assignments on the planet.

The emotions often braided with grief are frequently talked about as steps, even though grief is not navigated in a linear fashion, nor is the journey through it the same for everyone. Anyone who has grieved unimaginable loss will tell you it is not a step-taking or stage-navigating process but rather an effort to hold your ground despite crashing waves that vary in strength and timing of arrival. If you go with an expanded version of a grief journey description, the seven stages are shock and denial, pain and guilt, anger and bargaining, depression, the upward turn, reconstruction and working through, and acceptance and hope.[3] The list of emotions, however, are universally identified among those that arrive when someone experiences a loss. There is no way to live life without loss, so we all experience it; we just may not recognize how we as a society use sports to process and express it.

Cuts

One of the most emotional experiences families have with youth sports are tryouts and cuts. Being cut can either light a fire or extinguish one, and parents know that. Part of what determines how well an athlete will react to a cut depends on the emotion-processing behaviors they observe in their parents. They will either be elated or grief-stricken, and both emotions require mature navigation.

When an athlete is cut, denial can be one of the emotions that arrives. Denial is described as a "defense mechanism in which an individual refuses to recognize or acknowledge objective facts or experiences. It's an unconscious process that serves to protect the person from discomfort or anxiety."[4] I suppose it is appropriate to have this as one of the oft-accepted launching points of the grief journey. It's shock. It evokes resistance. People don't want to believe it at first.

As it relates to youth sports, denial can look like delusion or blame laying. Pursuit of a too lofty goal of achievement when talent does not support such a goal can take some people a long time to acknowledge. When athletes are young and the cut process is connected to decisions by other parents, it is very easy to argue they got it wrong. And maybe they did, but the truth of a child's athleticism will pan out over years, even though most parents want the validation and achievement right away.

Admittedly, I had a moment of such cut denial when I wrote a blog about our son being cut from a hockey team when he was twelve.[5] Being cut created an intimate grief that I hesitated to share, but it was the first time I had faced something like that, and I was already writing posts related to research for this book. I knew it was vulnerable to post my thoughts about it, and I never edited it, but as I look back at it a decade later, I read in my writing the denial and blame laying. I was told in not so many words that my reflections were not meant to be publicly shared and I should just keep those sentiments in a journal. Grief expression may come from a place of one emotion but invoke a separate emotion from someone else. I was sad. The man who told me to keep my thoughts private became angry.

I think the offering up of sadness and receiving it back as anger actually aligns with what a grief journey process might look and sound like in the sports context. You see grieving people lash out all the time. It is only now in hindsight I can see which response might have been more helpful to me. An acknowledgment of my sadness maybe would have been a good start. The thing is, he and I were parenting children at the same phase in life. We were in our late thirties and early forties, with kids entering the gauntlet of preteen drama. I was not mature enough to better express beyond my emotions, and he felt attacked as an evaluator for the tryout. We were of no use to one another. I found some solace in the reactions of friends who were experiencing the same cut emotions, and you see that alignment often when any teams are made. Those relegated to a lesser team are often together in disgruntled agreement that the world is against them and decisions cannot possibly be tied to the actual level of athleticism of their child. Working through the grief would serve all of them and their children much better.

LOSSES

Minor losses, and obviously the most common, happen when teams lose games. Those losses can become increasingly heavy as people endure losing seasons or find themselves involved in downtrodden programs. The loss of important games or tight contests can feel more intense than a regular-season loss. All of them tap at that inclination to grieve. More major losses are not really tangible and generally not as readily up for discussion. They can be tied to the loss of relationships, loss of status, or loss of a community when people are forced out or the clock runs out on their involvement.

When my husband was an assistant coach for a AAA hockey team in Colorado, our kids were very little. I became close friends with the wife of the head coach. She told me once, "You will lose friends if your kids play sports long enough." I didn't completely understand what she meant at the time, but as she tried to explain it to me, she talked about talent gaps that become chasms and relationships that, when too closely built on a shared sports experience, do not survive the natural progression that happens when some kids make it to the next level while others slowly move into doing other things. Her boys both played Division I and professional hockey, and both are now high-level college and pro coaches. Many of the families with whom they shared the youth years of their development severed ties when it was clear they were not going to share the same path. Unfortunately, those losses of friendships are increasingly part of the sports landscape, especially for the elite and travel folks. If members of team adult harbor a desire to belong to a sports community and they find themselves floating through higher levels essentially alone, it can be grief-inducing.

Unfortunately, the lack of relationships isn't even as devastating as what can happen when forged relationships present themselves as friendships but are tied more closely to youth sports politics or status alignment. I met Greg, a father of five kids, when he was at the start of their family's youth sports journey. He was an energetic and enthusiastic man who had moved his family to a hub community precisely because of the sports offerings they could enjoy there. He coached a number of his children's teams in a couple different sports, and to even the most casual observer, he was obviously very passionate about sports. He and his family were a staple on baseball and football fields, as well as in hockey arenas.

I interviewed him seven years later, wanting to find out how things went for him and his children. At the time of the second interview, his oldest was out of high school and finishing up his first year in college. The others were in the middle of high school–sports craziness. I asked him what he learned from his time coaching all those teams and investing as much as he did into the youth sports experience. He took a deep breath, looked down at his hands, and said, "I found out who my real friends are. People were willing to be my friend for all the wrong reasons and then turn their back on me. Our oldest probably should have gone through counseling because of everything he had to go through. He endured the bullying, and we were eventually ostracized as a family."

When pressed for the details, he shared that, for the majority of his time coaching, the community seemed to rally behind him as a coach—that is, until the teams were divided for one season, and a small group of people blamed him for their kids' being relegated to a "lesser" team. A couple of seasons later, the father of one of those kids was in a position as an assistant coach for Greg's son. Revenge seemed to be on his agenda. Greg's son was bullied by the coach and by the players on the team, who were also classmates at school. It was relentless. The "natives" of this hub community (people who were born there and had stronger roots) were not going to accept Greg's outside energy or budding, athletic children, and the pushback against what they had initially accepted was devastating to the family. Most of Greg's kids ended up changing schools and playing for other communities. Despite wanting to be part of a robust sports community, Greg and his family found out how potentially destructive the wrong chemistry of people can become and the deep levels of grief they've had to navigate as a result.

Mourning expectations took on an entirely new level for Jenna and her family. As a junior in high school, Jenna had been invited to be on the roster of a Division I team. She was very excited about what she thought was the commitment she had worked so hard to attain. The summer after her senior year, her parents booked hotels in all the cities the team was scheduled to play that next fall, while Jenna got busy preparing for the season with workouts and training. Eight weeks before she was slated to report to training camp, there was a coaching change for the program, and she received word that her offer had been rescinded and they no longer had a spot for her on the team.

Her mom described it as devastating. They had expected to send Jenna to this school and had planned all their fall travel around her games, and whatever they had envisioned for the next few years vanished in an instant. There was a lot to grieve with that one: loss of trust in promises, loss of plans and expectations, and loss of identity without a place to call home. Eventually they were able to get her connected with a team who had recruited her the year before she signed, and she ended up playing Division I, but the entire experience scarred them all.

Because of the stories people shared with me during my research, I was able to quickly identify the grief that arrived for me when my husband decided he could no longer coach high school hockey. I was sure his resignation was the decision that would ostracize us. "No high school sports community for me," I thought. It was an unfounded fear, but it was important that I spent time coming to terms with the "loss" of what I had expected.

INJURIES

Our daughter Haley had a devastating knee injury at the start of her hockey season in eighth grade. She dislocated her kneecap, chipped a bone, and damaged the ligaments that work to hold the kneecap in place. I was pissed.

No one had touched her, and the entire thing unfolded in dramatic fashion at a meaningless practice at the start of what we expected would be a positive and successful season. It ended in an instant. And then we were heading into surgery, recovery, and the unknown future of her time playing. I had been in that very uncomfortable space before as an athlete, and her injury brought back emotions I hadn't realized I had yet to let go. I was carrying anger connected to my personal grief and standing face to face with an angry, grieving preteen child. We were poised for conflict.

Grief presents in a number of ways when injuries sideline athletes. Most of the time it is tied to a loss of expectation. Plans, trips, and hopes about participation are instantly changed. Athletes are relegated to the training room, families have to shuffle schedules to accommodate doctor and physical therapy appointments, and staying engaged with the team and team activities gets harder or doesn't happen at all. Grief and often anger because of those losses arrive for both the athlete and the parents. It's upsetting.

It is really important to acknowledge and work through the arrival of ugly emotions like anger that arrive when grief does. *Psychology Today* explains, "Anger is one of the basic human emotions, as elemental as happiness, sadness, anxiety, or disgust. . . . Prolonged release of the stress hormones that accompany anger can destroy neurons in areas of the brain associated with judgment and short-term memory, and weaken the immune system."[6] I knew it was not a good thing that I had been carrying anger that bubbled when our daughter got hurt. I set to work on myself, journaling to process my own grief and seeking out ways to help her work through hers. Thankfully, I was a better version of myself when we navigated several years of injury with our youngest while she was in high school. Parenting athletes has meant constant work through grief for me so I can better help my children to get through their own grief-inducing moments.

ENDINGS

Endings are inevitable. We cannot avoid them, and sometimes they sneak up on us well before we are ready. No one really knows the sports story a child will live until it has been fully written. One thing I know with 100 percent certainty is that the story will end. And for 99.9 percent of those stories, negative emotions are at least part of what people feel when it does. Our kids decided sports had served them long enough and ended their competitive sports stories their senior years in high school, even though I had been prepared to cheer for them longer. Our oldest could have pursued Division III soccer, but he wanted to go to UW-Madison. Pond hockey, pickup basketball, and video games are what he plays now. Our middle daughter could have played hockey as a D-III goalie, but she wanted to pursue nursing and was ready to focus all her energy on that. Pickleball is her game of choice these days. Our youngest also could have played Division III soccer, but a second knee injury at the start of her senior year gave her the goal to simply play one more high school season. She and I will share her final season together. Each of our kids played sports until the year they turned eighteen. Youth sports mission complete.

I have coached high school soccer for eight years. I've been on the field with eight classes of seniors and their parents, who arrive at that ending in a number of ways. I've watched some people navigate the waters of sports-story grief well, and I've watched others flail in the heavy and heart-challenging emotions.

My sincere invitation to all parents who have navigated the sports journey to the end with their kids is that they give themselves the space they deserve to grieve that ending, too. I wrote a letter like this to one of my friends and gave it to her on her son's senior night:

Dear Senior Parent:

I know tonight's Senior Night is their night, but I want to give you a nod, too. Whether they can verbalize it to you or not, I know you have loved them fiercely. I have seen your passion for the games they played and your support of the struggles they've endured. We all know this sports journey is so much bigger than your presence on the sideline of this final game. You have poured yourself out for them and cheered louder and bigger than anyone else could. They got to this point because of you and everything you've offered up to them is now at the core of who they are. It will be what they take with them everywhere they go from now on. It's OK to let them go now. You've done good!

Now, if you are ultra-sad, angry, anxious, or depressed about any sort of ending, then it is probable you have some grief work to do. Bernard Golden, a psychotherapist in anger management, writes, "Suppressed grief can lead to chronic emotional numbness, low-level depression, diminished energy, and an overall reduction in motivation."[7] We tell our kids to keep pushing because they can do hard things. We can, too. Aiming for a level of acceptance about all the grief-evoking experiences should be our goal.

Without meaning to draw out the timeline for this project, I am grateful I had ten years to uncover and then work through the material I collected. When I'd have an unexpected emotion arrive, like being angry with my daughter for getting hurt, I put it under a deconstructionist microscope. I still carried plenty of grief about my dad, but the work I put in to be better for my daughter helped me to let go of the anger I harbored for him, too. Letting go of that anger allowed me to see him in a new light, and with that perspective, I was open to a new way of looking at him I didn't initially see coming.

I learned about chronic traumatic encephalopathy (CTE) at a concussion symposium in 2019. As I listened to the observed behaviors of athletes who were later determined to have suffered from CTE, I connected the dots about my dad's entire life story: dramatic personality shift, chronic alcoholism, loss of executive function, and ultimately severe dementia. I brought my suspicions to my mom and siblings, and they agreed to journey with me to donate my dad's brain to the Boston University brain bank when he died. The clinical physicians interviewed us extensively, and the pathologists looked at his brain in depth. The findings revealed that, of four levels, our dad had level 3 CTE. Because of his time as a small, running quarterback through high school and on the 150-pound team at West Point, probable repeated head impacts irreparably damaged his brain. He will forever be a legacy donor for the CTE Legacy Foundation, where his life story has been memorialized on their legacy stories page. A new grief emerged with that news, but I was also able to let go of some of the other pain I felt because of unfulfilled expectations.

I don't know what might be the grief that lives in your cells, and I have no way of knowing if you have absorbed it healthfully or not. If you struggle to control emotions while watching your children play sports, especially the most vicious emotion, anger, then you would do yourself and your children a true service to explore what losses or endings you have not fully processed and work through the grief that may linger.

Golden hits it on the head when he says, "What we don't acknowledge controls us—and being held hostage by anger may only postpone the rawness of grief." I wholeheartedly agree with his assessment, "Our well-being depends on our resilience to grieve."[8] Give yourself that permission.

Processing Grief

- Acknowledge its presence.
- Identify its possible source(s).
- Work to identify the emotion(s) that arrive with it.
- Let yourself feel those hard feelings.
- Write through or talk through it. Focus on the feelings, not necessarily the circumstances that evoked it.
- Let yourself cry, punch a pillow, or run a sprint if you need to physically express it.
- Repeat as needed.
- Seek professional input if you are not able to mitigate grief on your own.

CHAPTER 12

Positively Peace Filled

Personally, in Your Family, and on the Sidelines

"I'M DONE COACHING HIGH SCHOOL HOCKEY," MY HUSBAND TOLD me as we followed our chiweenie on a morning walk in early spring. He kept his eyes to the ground, and we walked in silence as I absorbed his statement. He had just finished his third season as the varsity coach, and I had just started as the boys' soccer coach at the same high school.

In my head, coaching was a beautiful way for us both to give back to the games that built us; to engage positively in the community we had finally decided to call home; and to have a chance to spend special time with our son, who was a sophomore in both programs. There was a lot going through my head, including the fact that my husband's high school coaching gig was one of the main reasons we had moved back to town—for the third time (don't ask; we were trying to figure out our lives).

"I just can't do it anymore," he said. "I have a day job, and coaching high school is way more stressful than I have energy to deal with."

I knew what he meant. Despite all my positive spouse coaching as he debriefed about practices, games, parent phone calls, angry emails, sharing athletes with the football program, and the overall demands of people who expected more from a season than they were willing to prepare for in the off-season, I did not have a way to remove all that was too stressful for him. His stint as the coach was not what he had expected. He had imagined the boys and their families were passionate and devoted hockey people, the sort of passion and devotion he had come to know as a high school player in Minnesota. He hadn't imagined there would be a less-intense way to participate in high school hockey, and he was honestly ill prepared for a mindset he had never considered. There were a few completely dedicated folks, but hockey was the second or third "fun" sport for a large percentage of the players involved. There were entirely too many misaligned priorities between my husband and the families he was being asked to serve.

"Knowing I'm done will give me such peace of mind," he said.

I was the one who needed to find a way to join him where he had already landed. What felt like a sudden change in life plan did not evoke a peace-filled state of mind for me. I think I could say it was practically the opposite of peace. His proclamation made me feel distressed, discontented, and very uncomfortable.

Family member choices and experiences complicate our personal journeys. We cannot help but to feel pushed and pulled by the decisions, feelings, behaviors, and actions of those around us, especially when impactful decisions belong to those with whom we are most intimate. They are then further complicated by what we know happens with people's assumption that one person's actions are those that should be connected to an entire family. When we are part of a family, the stories of our family members affect the personal ones we write.

In an instant, my story was being written by someone other than me. To be honest, that happened with every autonomous decision our children made, too. Every mistake or misstep they navigated as they matured became woven into my story, too. Until that point, my husband and I had been aligned in the decisions we had made about our involvement in sports. We cheered for each other's coaching opportunities, and we showed up in support as a spouse should, making meals during seasons and holding down the fort for the one who grabbed the coaching whistle that day. His decision to stop coaching in the environment I was choosing rocked me.

I had been trying to connect with the hockey parents, but I found it difficult the season both the guys in my house were on the same bench. No matter how objectively I knew my husband was coaching, the opinions about his decisions were always there. Small groups of parents cannot help but to bounce around their opinions of a coach's choices, pointing out the decisions they would not have made. Either they forgot I was within earshot or, if they saw me in time, would abruptly shift and indicate to their listeners with eye movement that they needed to stop talking just then. Coaches' spouses attend games differently than most other adults who go. It can be a lonely seat to occupy and an interesting place to forge friendships. Add in the role of parent of a player on that team, and it is a lot to navigate with practically no control over any of it.

I knew my husband's departure was going to throw me into a new social space that I didn't really want to inhabit. I wasn't sure I could handle navigating the opinions of families in the program. They would either feel frustrated, angry, or sad because of his exit, or worse, they would feel elated he was gone.

"I don't care about their opinions," my husband said.

"That's the problem," I told him. "You aren't the one trying to foster relationships with people I would like to call my friends."

My head spun with thoughts about the ramifications of his decision for the community, the school in a department I had just joined, and the team his son still played for. I knew, too, our son, who had enjoyed his one opportunity to play for his dad, was going to need someone to walk beside him and he could use a peace-filled navigator. I was feeling everything but peace.

I did not want to stay in that mental or emotional state. The first place I went to start working through how it was making me feel was the one place that has marched me through unsettling circumstances my entire life: prayer. Very specifically the Serenity Prayer:

God, grant me the serenity
To accept the things I cannot change,
Courage to change the things I can,
And wisdom to know the difference.[1]

It's a simple prayer that has hung on my wall, been taped inside sports lockers, and moved me through distress more consistently than any other tool I have attempted to deploy. Thinking more critically about its effect for me, I know that serenity about letting go of those things out of my control offered the antidote to discontent. Very often what steals serenity, and it turns out not just for me but for most people, is focusing too heavily on what others think of me. So many decisions we make around community, including sports communities, come down to our built-in drive to obtain approval or respect from others. We pursue status above serenity.

Seeking wisdom about what is in our control (our beliefs about ourselves) and what is outside our control (what others believe about us) can profoundly shift our energy. "If you're motivated by 'What will others think of me?'" argues psychologist Michael Hurd, "then, to that extent, you're less likely to be motivated by the things that motivate capable, productive, innovative" people. He goes on to write, "An internal locus of control person wishes to use his or her thinking mind to figure out what makes sense, what works, what will do the thing he or she wishes to accomplish, or create, in reality. An external locus of control person is concerned more about the 'politics' of it all."[2] Youth sports challenge the emotions of adults because we convince ourselves that our peace depends on our children's achievements. Status is outside us, and serenity is within. The two are easily jumbled.

Let's do a little exercise. Think about your experiences in and around youth sports. Can you picture a moment of status (podium, roster designation, etc.)? Easy, right? What about peaceful moments? That's harder, isn't it? One of the last things we think about when we think about our engagement in competitive environments is experiencing any level of peace.

Peace is more than joy, pride, and elation, although all those emotions generally show up, too. We watched a high school player hit her one-thousandth point in a basketball game. Everyone in the gym knew it was coming, and anyone who had watched her battle over the years as a youth player knew how hard she had worked for that moment. The exhale at the three-pointer swish was a pride-filled moment for sure, but there was something else in her facial expression. She was relieved. She was at peace. As an adult watching her, I was, too. It was a pinnacle moment that marked the completion of a goal she had pursued and then achieved.

If you're like me or my husband, then you might point to instances when you finally accomplished a goal, or the kids in your care did, that left you with a sense of peace. Those were the experiences we noted when we talked about it. It's those big-sigh-of-relief exhales where contentment and peace live, but we don't experience it much when we are in the middle of working toward something. As we walk beside children on their sports-story journeys, most of the time there is little in the way of full "completion" or "achievement," and although hard to remember, it is all completely out of our control.

That's what is unnerving and makes it so hard to seek and find peace in our adult roles in the youth sports context. The peaceful zone is hard to create on a sports sideline. What are you, as the adult, really able to accomplish? How can you pursue peace in a space that is the opposite of conducive to it? And let's be honest, some sidelines are harder than others. Peace seeking is for churches or monasteries or a yurt in the woods. It usually needs to be a space where an emotional battle isn't happening right in front of you or inside you. It takes an interdisciplinary approach to bring about peace. Let's tackle it through a few of the abstract "ologies," like psychology, sociology, and theology (biological balance is necessary, too, but that is covered in chapter 9).

Positive Psychology

I discovered Martin Seligman's positive psychology theory while researching for my first book about marriage.[3] He was among one of the first psychologists to propose a focus on the effect of positivity on a person's ability to flourish. Much of my Choosing-to-Grow work as a parent, spouse, and coach has used suggestions and exercises borne out of Seligman's insights. Jeremy Sutton explains,

> The PERMA model is Seligman's framework for understanding and measuring wellbeing. [It] proposes we can break down wellbeing into five key elements: Positive emotions, Engagement, Relationships, Meaning, and Accomplishment. . . . The individual pursuing these elements becomes more able to deal with life's challenges. It becomes possible to create more meaningful lives with a powerful positive impact on increasing wellbeing while at the same time reducing psychological distress.[4]

Positive psychology is an incredibly powerful approach to life, including as a parent or coach in the youth sports arena.

It was rather unintentional how I learned about the Positive Coaching Alliance (PCA) and the work they are doing to bring positive psychology to the youth sports environment. I had posted my youth sports survey on Facebook and Twitter to garner as many varied responses as I could collect. As responses were coming in, I received a direct message inviting me into a conversation about circulating the survey among the membership of the PCA who had taken part in their training. I hadn't heard of the PCA, but the many resources and evidence-based approaches they were using to bring positive psychology to parents, coaches, and athletes quickly resonated with me.

We decided to partner in my research, and the PCA distributed the survey among some who had been trained through their programming. We wanted to see if there were any remarkable differences between how PCA-developed people responded compared to how the Twitter, Facebook, and my huddle participants were responding.

The PCA-only survey was a small sampling of about fifty people, and a few of their demographic characteristics would certainly affect their opinions: 70 percent of the respondents were men, compared to the general survey respondents, who were only 37 percent men; 81 percent of the PCA crew had more than six years of coaching experience, compared to only 37 percent of the general public responders. They were older too. While 60 percent of the social media responders were between the ages of thirty-six and forty-five, nearly 70 percent of the PCA participants were older than forty-six.

So the PCA crew was older; more experienced; and, I would argue, wiser given the level of play they generally had and the amount of coaching they had done. With all that wisdom, I expected there would be areas in the survey that stood out to me as measurable differences from the general public. I was right. On the question about the three most important traits of a "good team parent," 65 percent of the PCA respondents chose "supports the coach." The general public agreed that supporting the coach was important, but only 56 percent concurred. Arguably the most profound difference between the two groups had to do with a positive outlook. Only 44 percent of the general public felt as if "youth sports were moving in a positive direction," as opposed to 70 percent of those trained by PCA.

Whether PCA-trained folks were more positive to begin with or the training had an effect to help frame their opinions positively I cannot accurately assess. However, given the feedback and having employed several PCA resources for the last ten years, I am confident about its potential to positively affect all those exposed to the positive psychology it promotes.

One other interesting difference in the survey data was the three words they chose for "good team coach": 75 percent of the PCA responders chose teacher, while only 53 percent of the general public chose that. It's likely many of the PCA responders actually were teachers, but I would argue their involvement in the PCA influenced their perspective about the learning environment of youth sports, too. Growth mindset and learning focus are tenets of positive psychology and paramount to the training and resources PCA distributes.

I met Jim Thompson, founder of the PCA and author of *The Double-Goal Coach, Elevating Your Game,* and *Positive Sports Parenting*, when he was in the Twin Cities for the Youth Sports University Program. During his presentation, he said that youth sports provide an "endless procession of teachable moments." Creating and fostering a growth mindset for athletes, parents, and coaches changes the energy around the experience. If everyone is learning all the time, then there is hope. That positive atmosphere can create space for peace, while more contentious situations cannot.

Interviewing families twice over the course of seven years helped confirm the power of positive thinking. Those parents who told their initial stories with more positive language like "We hope," "I look forward to," and "We're excited about" ultimately had more positive stories the second time I interviewed them, too. Choosing the positive outlook seemed to significantly influence the sports stories they helped their children write. That positive outcome was not dependent on the athletic ability or the ultimate achievement of their children. The positive perspective operated independently of their circumstances. Either because their sports stories were positive or they had worked to reframe their experiences positively, they had chosen more positive emotions, one of

Seligman's elements. It allowed them to portray more emotional wisdom.

Emotional wisdom or emotional discipline marks the pinnacle of sports-parent maturity. The sooner you achieve that, the sooner you will enjoy peace in the experience, no matter what level of competition your children achieve. Seasoned parents know this. Similar to asking people at the end of their life, "What mattered most?" I asked seasoned sports parents what wisdom they wished they could share with their younger selves. Several of them echoed what Kevin said best. Kevin, the father of two professional hockey players who had twenty-five years' coaching experience, sixteen of which had been as a parent/coach, told me, "I wish I would have stepped back and enjoyed it more. Now when our boys play, I sit at the top of the rink, put my feet up, and enjoy the game, because I can't control anything. If you think about it, we didn't really control anything then, either. Your kids have to love it. It would have been nice to sit back and put my feet up then, too." He was enjoying a level of peace he wished he had found earlier in the journey.

For those who struggle to positively think their way out of difficult emotions, I encourage thoughtful consideration of a form of therapy that could also prove helpful. It is called acceptance commitment therapy. Introduced by psychology professor and author Steven C. Hayes, it is a practice in steps to make purposeful use of the emotions that arrive. He writes, "The new emphasis is on learning to step back from what you are thinking, notice it, and open up to what you are experiencing. These steps keep us from doing the damage to ourselves that efforts to avoid or control our thoughts or feelings inflict, allowing us to focus our energies on taking the positive actions that can alleviate our suffering."[5] Learning to understand the power we can enact over the emotions that do not serve us can get us closer to the peace that benefits us.

SOCIOLOGY

It's worth pursuing inner peace because it is what leads to flourishing. Juan Xi, who received her PhD in medical sociology, and Matthew Lee, the director of the Human Flourishing Program at Harvard, conducted research related to inner peace. They write, "The state of inner peace may be present in all life circumstances, including challenging or disturbing situations." Their findings suggest that those who are able to achieve inner peace have three discernible traits and ways of thinking. People who have inner peace have a "skillful ability to accept the inevitable losses that are an inherent part of the human condition, [avoid] undue fixation on transitory pleasures and things, [and] foster a calm and balanced mind."[6] They do argue that the three characteristics are likely dynamically linked. The acceptance of loss and not worrying about material pursuit can actually be influenced by calming and balancing the mind first. You will not find peace if your energy is spent seeking wins and status.

Without really planning, I have spent my life walking this path toward serenity, laying down tracks of acceptance and courage each time I uttered that prayer, invoking two of the three things Xi and Lee note are necessary to achieving inner peace. It is a path that can only be carved out by taking intentional steps and is essentially the definition of Choosing to Grow. Xi and Lee explain, "Being well is more than just being free from problems. And people grow from dealing with their problems and achieve higher levels of well-being." They go on to write, "It is not avoidance or indifference. Individuals make efforts to find and maintain inner balance or equanimity rather than passively follow the default mental model, which tends to produce automatic reactions to stimuli in the environment (e.g., perceive a threat, feel the fear, and react with avoidance)."[7] Working to heal is worthy. You have to choose whether you would prefer to be on a different path than one of discontent and strife. Then you must take intentional steps to work toward peace. That generally means you have to do uncomfortable and difficult work worthy of wise guidance.

THEOLOGY

Do you have a role model for peace? To where do you turn for insight or wisdom? Faith and religion offer space for this conversation, and many of the world's religions are founded on the same tenets.

The Dalai Lama, a Tibetan Buddhist, proports otherworldly or transcendent mentality. He instructs Buddhists to guard their inner peace by not being influenced by the behavior of others. It is an invitation to be above the happenings of the world, in line with a call for followers of Buddhism to detach themselves from worldly cravings. Pema Chodron, a famous American Tibetan Buddhist, has said, "Inner peace begins the moment you choose not to allow another person or event to control your emotions."[8] Buddhists cannot achieve enlightenment without inner peace.

Followers of Judaism are mandated to "seek peace and pursue it."[9] The Torah is a source of their peace.[10] Christians attain peace through Jesus. The invitation to follow his teachings instructs people to love. One of Jesus's followers wrote this description of what it takes to love: "Love is patient; love is kind; love is not envious or boastful or arrogant or rude. It does not insist on its own way; it is not irritable; it keeps no records of wrongs; it does not rejoice in wrongdoing but rejoices in truth. It bears all things, believes all things, hopes all things, endures all things."[11]

Love is to will the good of the other, and were adults to adopt the posture of love with all kids playing youth sports, we'd be able to achieve peace on the fields, in the rinks, and on the courts. It would happen each time a child was afforded the chance to play, given an opportunity to learn as they compete, and encouraged to grow toward their potential. It's actually a lot simpler than we make it.

Can you even visualize how profoundly different the youth sports environment would feel if all the adults showed up with the intent to embody the description of love or to be in full pursuit of the described offerings of peace? People could still be loud, engaged, enthusiastic, and colorful, but what inner peace affords them is an opportunity to become the fertile landing spot and the positive presence growing kids need. The more inner peace you have, the more peace you have at your disposal to offer to others.

PEACE IN RELATIONSHIPS DEPENDS ON POSITIVE COMMUNICATION

We can have profound influence on the people with whom we engage. What we share, how we share it, and what we receive affects and develops all the relationships in our lives. Dawn O. Braithwaite, a professor of communication, writes, "In communication, we develop, create, maintain, and alter our relationships. As we communicate, we become and change who we are. . . . We co-create relationships and our own identity."[12] Coming into a conversation with a level head, a balanced thought process, and in a peaceful state of mind will absolutely influence the level of peace in the room and in our relationships.

Have you thought about your influence as it relates to the spheres in which you operate? You engage in small circles of influence in your familial relationships, and then the circles expand in size from there. If you are a teacher, then your sphere extends to your students; if you are a business owner, then it extends to your employees or peers; if you are a coach or an administrator, then your sphere expands to all the people for whom your decisions matter. Are the spheres you occupy contentious or peaceful? What effect can you have in the opportunities you are given? As a parent, coach, spouse of a coach, board member, grandparent, or a fan raising children in the sporting context, bringing a level of peace, calm, and positivity will influence people with whom you engage, if even on a very small scale.

I wasn't the one to decide that my husband was done coaching. I hadn't made any of the decisions while he was coaching, and I couldn't control the fallout of his choice. What I could do was work toward my personal peace and then show up in the public sphere willing to share as positively as I could.

BECOME BETTER COMMUNICATORS

If the emotional distress you carry needs to be worked out with someone else, then you can and should control the strategies you employ. The communication strategy that will ultimately diffuse the most tension is to use "I" statements: "I feel ____" instead of "You are so ____," "You must ____," or "You have to ____." Stick with completing the sentence "I feel ____," and then ask a question in order to clarify how the other person feels. Do this with the intention to listen to the answer.

Active listening is the other half of good communication. Active listeners listen with their entire bodies. They make eye contact, they think about how receptive their body posture is, and they focus entirely on the person speaking and push out any thoughts that are not coming from the speaker. Very often people appear as though they are listening when they are really formulating their responses while you speak. Active listeners are good at conveying to the speaker what they heard that person say.

SIDELINES

Every human experience can be framed the way we train our brains to frame it. We can view losses as learning opportunities and conflict as a way to grow, and we absolutely have the capacity to show up on a sideline with the intention to remain peace filled and to offer a positive space for the kids to do their best growing. We'll be at our peace-filled best if we are authentically pursuing an enlightened mind, speaking and listening in positive and constructive ways, and viewing those around us as part of a community with whom positive engagement matters.

We need youth sports for all the lessons they teach, as well as the exercise and camaraderie they offer. Building our next generation of adults will depend on our willingness to improve the tools we offer. Social division is rising; high levels of negative emotions are rampant; and fresh air, fun, games, movement for physical health, and access to the challenges that grow physical, emotional, and mental muscles are the necessary antidotes. Youth sports need to be and do better for all kids, and it is up to team adult to make it happen. We can do that by learning to love them well, being willing to love one another, finding a way to love the process, and making the most of the opportunities we're given to positively journey through all of it.

Notes

Introduction

1. Susan Eustis, "Youth Sports Market Grows," WinterGreen Research, updated August 10, 2023, https://www.wintergreenresearch.com/post/youth-sports-market-grows.

2. Research and Markets, "Youth Sports Market Projected to Reach $77.6 Billion by 2026—Comprehensive Industry Analysis and Insights," GlobeNewswire, December 26, 2019, https://www.globenewswire.com/news-release/2019/12/26/1964575/0/en/Youth-Sports-Market-Projected-to-Reach-77-6-Billion-by-2026-Comprehensive-Industry-Analysis-Insights.html.

3. Andy Cerda, "Family Time Is Far More Important than Other Aspects of Life for Most Americans," Pew Research Center, May 26, 2023, https://www.pewresearch.org/short-reads/2023/05/26/family-time-is-far-more-important-than-other-aspects-of-life-for-most-americans/.

Chapter 1

1. Quoted in Jamie D. Aten, "What Is Joy and What Does It Say about Us?" *Psychology Today*, July 28, 2020, https://www.psychologytoday.com/us/blog/hope-resilience/202007/what-is-joy-and-what-does-it-say-about-us.

2. Vanessa LoBue, "What Our Faces Say to Our Children," *Psychology Today*, September 14, 2020, https://www.psychologytoday.com/us/blog/the-baby-scientist/202009/what-our-faces-say-our-children.

3. Quoted in Jane Collingwood, "Teaching Your Baby Sign Language Can Benefit Both of You," PsychCentral, May 17, 2016, https://www.psychcentral.com/lib/teaching-your-baby-sign-language-can-benefit-both-of-you#1.

4. Johns Hopkins Medicine, "The Benefits of Playing with Your Child," accessed May 21, 2024, https://www.hopkinsmedicine.org/health/wellness-and-prevention/the-benefits-of-playing-with-your-child.

5. Colin Higgs, Richard Way, Vicki Harber, Paul Jurbala, and Istvan Balyi, *Long-Term Development in Sport and Physical Activity 3.0* (Victoria, BC: Sport

for Life, 2019), https://sportforlife.ca/wp-content/uploads/2019/06/Long-Term -Development-in-Sport-and-Physical-Activity-3.0.pdf.

6. Project Play, "Children's Bill of Rights in Sports," Aspen Institute, accessed May 21, 2024, https://projectplay.org/childrens-rights-and-sports.

7. Paul J. McCarthy, Marc V. Jones, and David Clark-Carter, "Understanding Enjoyment in Youth Sport: A Developmental Perspective," *Psychology of Sport and Exercise* 9, no. 2 (March 2008): 142–56, https://doi.org/10.1016/j.psychsport .2007.01.005.

8. John Wilson, "That's Why They Call It Play: The Joy of Sports," filmed May 15, 2014, in Charleston, SC, TED video, 10:17, https://youtu.be/ra7uJtVj1bI?si =LxNS5VGkCUDTYCgj.

9. Milken Institute School of Public Health, "Amanda J. Visek," George Washington University, accessed May 21, 2024, https://publichealth.gwu.edu/ departments/exercise-and-nutrition-sciences/amanda-visek.

10. Amanda J. Visek, Heather Mannix, Avinash Chandran, Sean D. Cleary, Karen A. McDonnell, and Loretta DiPietro, "Toward Understanding Youth Athletes' Fun Priorities: An Investigation of Sex, Age, and Levels of Play," *Women in Sport and Physical Activity Journal* 28, no. 1 (April 2020): 34–49, https: //doi.org/10.1123/wspaj.2018-0004.

11. Lindsey Wilson, "The Lifelong Pursuit of Joy in Sports," *Positive Performance Training* (blog), June 1, 2022, https://www.positiveperformancetraining .com/blog/the-lifelong-pursuit-of-cultivating-joy-in-sports.

CHAPTER 2

1. Massachusetts General Hospital and Harvard Medical School, "Harvard Second Generation Study," accessed June 13, 2024, https://www .adultdevelopmentstudy.org/.

2. Saul Mcleod, "Maslow's Hierarchy of Needs," Simply Psychology, updated January 24, 2024, https://www.simplypsychology.org/maslow.html.

3. George Vaillant, "Your Childhood Is Crucial to How You'll Age," Next Avenue, October 31, 2013, https://www.nextavenue.org/why-your-childhood -crucial-how-youll-age/.

4. *Oxford Learner's Dictionaries*, "Pride," accessed May 21, 2024, https://www .oxfordlearnersdictionaries.com/definition/english/pride_1.

5. *Merriam-Webster.com Dictionary*, "Pride," accessed May 21, 2024, https:// www.merriam-webster.com/dictionary/pride.

6. Jessica L. Tracy, "Pride: It Brings Out the Best—and Worst—in Humans," *Scientific American*, November 1, 2013, https://www.scientificamerican.com/ article/pride-it-brings-out-the-best-and-worst-in-humans/.

7. Lisa Firestone, "Is Being Proud of Your Kids Really about You?" *Psychology Today*, June 14, 2017, https://www.psychologytoday.com/us/blog/compassion -matters/201706/is-being-proud-your-kids-really-about-you.

8. Tracy, "Pride."

9. Jessica L. Tracy. *Pride: The Secret of Success* (New York: HarperCollins, 2016).

10. St. Thomas Aquinas, *Summa of Theology I*, Q20 A1 ad. 3.

Chapter 3

1. *A League of Their Own*, directed by Penny Marshall (Culver City, CA: Columbia Pictures, 1993).

2. Alia Hoyt, "How Crying Works," HowStuffWorks, updated June 9, 2023, https://science.howstuffworks.com/life/inside-the-mind/emotions/crying.htm.

3. Lauren Camera, "More Americans Say Transgender Athletes Should Only Play for Teams That Match Gender of Birth," *U.S. News & World Report*, July 13, 2023, https://www.usnews.com/news/national-news/articles/2023-06-13/more-americans-say-transgender-athletes-should-only-play-for-teams-that-match-gender-at-birth.

4. Quoted in Rosalind Franklin University, "Massive Study Reveals Few Differences between Men and Women's Brains," Neuroscience News, March 25, 2021, https://neurosciencenews.com/brain-sex-differences-18107/.

5. Lutz Jäncke, "Sex/Gender Differences in Cognition, Neurophysiology, and Neuroanatomy," *F1000Research* 7 (June 20, 2018): 805, https://doi.org/10.12688/f1000research.13917.1.

6. Scottie Andrew Fellow, "Five Ways High Testosterone Impacts Men's Behavior," *Newsweek*, updated July 9, 2018, https://www.newsweek.com/five-ways-high-testosterone-impacts-mens-behavior-1010705.

7. Lutz Jäncke, "Sex/Gender Differences in Cognition, Neurophysiology, and Neuroanatomy," *F1000Research* 7 (June 20, 2018): 805, https://doi.org/10.12688/f1000research.13917.1.

8. Maddie Koss, "No, They're Not Boys. But Madison Soccer Team Endures Criticism Because Players Have Short Hair," *Milwaukee Journal Sentinel*, August 5, 2017, https://www.jsonline.com/story/news/2017/08/05/madison-girls-soccer-team-bristles-critics-who-say-players-boys/459741001/.

9. Sebastian Ocklenburg, "13 Surprising Scientific Findings about Crying," *Psychology Today*, September 17, 2020, https://www.psychologytoday.com/us/blog/the-asymmetric-brain/202009/13-surprising-scientific-findings-about-crying.

10. Family Education, "What Boys Learn from Their Dads," accessed May 21, 2024, https://www.familyeducation.com/family-life/dad-life/what-boys-learn-their-dads.

11. June Gruber and Jessica L. Borelli, "The Importance of Fostering Emotional Diversity in Boys," *Scientific American*, December 12, 2017, https://www.scientificamerican.com/article/the-importance-of-fostering-emotional-diversity-in-boys/.

12. Scott Cacciola, "There Was Always Crying in Sports. The Kelces Made It Cool," *New York Times*, March 6, 2024, https://www.nytimes.com/2024/03/06/style/jason-kelce-crying.htm.

13. Clayton Ellis, Becky Foellmer, Mark Foellmer, Rick Howard, Robert Knipe, Ann Paulis-Neal, Lisa Paulson, and Allison Ross, *Physical Activity Should Not Be Used as Punishment and/or Behavior Management* (Annapolis Junction, MD: SHAPE, 2021), https://www.shapeamerica.org/Common/Uploaded%20files/uploads/2021/advocacy/position-statements/Physical-Activity-Should-Not-Be-Used-as-Punishment-and-or-Behavior-Management.pdf.

14. Rachel Simmons, *Odd Girl Out: The Hidden Culture of Aggression in Girls* (New York: Mariner Books, 2011); Rosalind Wiseman, *Queen Bees and Wannabes: Helping Your Daughter Survive Cliques, Gossip, Boys, and the New Realities of Girl World*, 3rd ed. (New York: Harmony Books, 2016).

Chapter 4

1. BVM Sportsdesk, "Minnesota Boys High School Hockey Championship Shines Brighter than NHL Games," BVM Sports, March 10, 2024, https://bvmsports.com/2024/03/10/minnesota-boys-high-school-hockey-championship-shines-brighter-than-nhl-games.

2. Minnesota Hockey, "Minnesota Hockey Replaces Residency Rule with Participation Rule," Rogers Youth Hockey Association, October 3, 2009, https://www.rogershockey.com/news_article/show/31348#.

3. Eric Higbee, "Why the Three Rings of Community Are So Important," The Answer Is Community, March 7, 2023, https://www.theansweris.community/the-three-rings-of-community-and-why-they-are-so-important/.

4. Marc J. Dunkelman, *The Vanishing Neighbor: The Transformation of American Community* (New York: W. W. Norton, 2014).

5. Higbee, "Three Rings of Community."

6. Data Commons, "Woodbury," accessed May 24, 2024, https://datacommons.org/place/geoId/2771428.

7. Emily Barone, "The Astronomical Cost of Kids' Sports," *Time*, August 24, 2017, https://time.com/4913284/kids-sports-cost/.

8. Project Play, "Youth Sports Facts: Challenges," Aspen Institute, accessed May 21, 2024, https://projectplay.org/youth-sports/facts/challenges.

9. Cassandra Coble and Richard Buning, "Why Massive New Youth Sports Facilities May Not Lead to the Tourist Boom Many Communities Hope for When They Build Them," Conversation, January 18, 2022, https://theconversation.com/why-massive-new-youth-sports-facilities-may-not-lead-to-the-tourist-boom-many-communities-hope-for-when-they-build-them-173126.

10. Project Play, "Youth Sports Facts."

11. United Nations Department of Economic and Social Affairs, "Addressing Climate Change through Sport," policy brief 128, January 2022, https://www.un.org/development/desa/dpad/wp-content/uploads/sites/45/PB_128.pdf.

12. Bryon Sheffield, "2023 Annual Soccer Parent Survey Report!" Soccer Parenting, January 22, 2024, https://www.soccerparenting.com/2023-annual-soccer -parent-survey-report/.

13. Shelley E. Taylor, "Tend and Befriend: Biobehavioral Bases of Affiliation under Stress." *Current Directions in Psychological Science* 15, no. 6 (December 2006): 273–77, https://www.jstor.org/stable/20183134.

CHAPTER 5

1. Kendra Cherry, "Motivation: The Driving Force behind Our Actions," Verywell Mind, updated May 3, 2023, https://www.verywellmind.com/what-is -motivation-2795378.

2. James Lehman, "How to Give Kids Consequences That Work," EmpoweringParents.com, accessed May 21, 2024, https://www.empoweringparents.com/ article/how-to-give-kids-consequences-that-work/.

3. Courtney E. Ackerman, "Self-Determination Theory and How It Explains Motivation," Positive Psychology, June 21, 2018, https://positivepsychology.com /self-determination-theory/.

4. Richard M. Ryan and Edward L. Deci, "Self-Determination Theory and the Facilitation of Intrinsic Motivation, Social Development, and Well-Being," *American Psychologist* 55, no. 1 (January 2000): 68–78, https://doi.org/10.1037// 0003-066x.55.1.68.

5. Istvan Balyi and Jim Grove, "If You're Raising a Child Athlete, Think Long-Term," Active for Life, March 11, 2013, https://activeforlife.com/raising -child-athlete-long-term/.

6. Delia O'Hara, "The Intrinsic Motivation of Richard Ryan and Edward Deci," American Psychological Association, 2017, https://www.apa.org/members /content/intrinsic-motivation.

7. O'Hara, "Intrinsic Motivation."

CHAPTER 6

1. Margo Mountjoy, Jorunn Sundgot-Borgen, Louise Burke, Susan Carter, Naama Constantini, Constance Lebrun, and Nanna Meyer, "The IOC Consensus Statement: Beyond the Female Athlete Triad—Relative Energy Deficiency in Sport (RED-S)," *British Journal of Sports Medicine* 48, no. 7 (April 2014): 491– 97, https://doi.org/10.1136/bjsports-2014-093502.

2. Mountjoy et al., "IOC Consensus Statement."

3. Robert S. Weinberg and Daniel Gould, *Foundations of Sport and Exercise Psychology*, 5th ed. (Champaign, IL: Human Kinetics, 2011), 447, 451.

4. Jim Taylor, "Develop Emotional Mastery in Your Young Athletes," *Psychology Today*, October 16, 2017, https://www.psychologytoday.com/us/blog/ the-power-prime/201710/develop-emotional-mastery-in-your-young-athletes.

5. DiveThru Team, "Feeling Hurt: A Guide to Your Emotions," DiveThru, updated January 26, 2023, https://divethru.com/feeling-hurt-a-guide-to-your-emotions/.

6. Elizabeth Hartney, "How Emotional Pain Affects Your Body," Verywell Mind, updated May 20, 2024, https://www.verywellmind.com/physical-pain-and-emotional-pain-22421.

7. Project Play, "Physical and Mental Health Trends," Aspen Institute, accessed May 21, 2024, https://projectplay.org/state-of-play-2022/physical-mental-health-trends.

CHAPTER 7

1. Rebecca Joy Stanborough, "Concrete Thinking: Building Block, Stumbling Block, or Both?" Healthline, August 30, 2019, https://www.healthline.com/health/concrete-thinking.

2. Cameron Anderson and John Angus D. Hildreth, *Striving for Superiority: The Human Desire for Status*, working paper 115–16 (Berkeley: University of California, October 2016), https://irle.berkeley.edu/wp-content/uploads/2016/10/Striving-for-superiority.pdf.

3. Anne H. Gauthier and Petra W. de Jong, "Costly Children: The Motivations for Parental Investment in Children in a Low Fertility Context," *Genus Journal of Population Sciences* 77, no. 6 (2021), https://doi.org/10.1186/s41118-020-00111-5.

4. Melanie Greenberg, "The Neuroscience of Fairness and Injustice," *Psychology Today*, August 22, 2014, https://www.psychologytoday.com/us/blog/the-mindful-self-express/201408/the-neuroscience-fairness-and-injustice.

5. Mark E. Feinberg, Anna R. Solmeyer, and Susan M. McHale, "The Third Rail of Family Systems: Sibling Relationships, Mental and Behavioral Health, and Preventive Intervention in Childhood and Adolescence," *Clinical Child and Family Psychology Review* 15, no. 1 (March 2012): 43–57, https://doi.org/10.1007/s10567-011-0104-5.

6. Feinberg, Solmeyer, and McHale, "Third Rail."

7. Vincent Iannelli, "When Should Puberty Start in Girls and Boys?" Verywell Family, updated April 5, 2022, https://www.verywellfamily.com/when-should-puberty-start-2632063.

8. Mark Zeigler, "Column: Norway's Hands-Off Approach to Youth Sports Might Explain Why They're So Good When They Get Older," *San Diego Union-Tribune*, July 20, 2022, https://www.sandiegouniontribune.com/sports/sports-columnists/story/2022-07-20/zeigler-norway-youth-sports-track-field-world-athletics-championships-eugene-karsten-warholm.

9. Dawn R. Matthias, letter to Joe Zydowsky, September 11, 2019, United States Department of Education Office for Civil Rights, https://www2.ed.gov/about/offices/list/ocr/docs/investigations/more/05171450-a.pdf.

10. Resolution Agreement, Menomonie Area School District, Office of Civil Rights case no. 05-17-1450, accessed May 21, 2024, https://www2.ed.gov/about/offices/list/ocr/docs/investigations/more/05171450-b.pdf.

11. Derek Thompson, "American Meritocracy Is Killing Youth Sports," *Atlantic*, November 6, 2018, https://www.theatlantic.com/ideas/archive/2018/11/income-inequality-explains-decline-youth-sports/574975/.

12. Dionne Koller and Han Xiao, *Passing the Torch: Modernizing Olympic, Paralympic, and Grassroots Sports in America* (n.p.: Commission on the State of U.S. Olympics & Paralympics 2024), https://www.csusop.org/.

13. Koller and Xiao, *Passing the Torch.*

14. McGregor Smyth, quoted in New York Lawyers for the Public Interest, "Court Approves Landmark Sports Equity Class Action Settlement, Increasing Access to Sports for Black and Latinx High School Students," press release, March 10, 2022, https://www.nylpi.org/court-approves-landmark-sports-equity-class-action-settlement-increasing-access-to-sports-for-black-and-latinx-high-school-students/.

15. Will Hobson, "The Fight for the Future of Transgender Athletes," *Washington Post*, April 15, 2021, https://www.washingtonpost.com/sports/2021/04/15/transgender-athletes-womens-sports-title-ix/.

16. Dan Roan and Katie Falkingham, "Transgender Athletes: What Do the Scientists Say?" BBC Sport, May 11, 2022, https://www.bbc.com/sport/61346517.

17. Marilou St-Pierre, "The Inclusion of Trans and Non-Binary People in Sport: It's a Matter for Everyone!" Sport for Life webinar, January 25, 2024.

CHAPTER 8

1. Shahram Heshmat, "Why Do People Drink?" *Psychology Today*, March 3, 2017, https://www.psychologytoday.com/us/blog/science-choice/201703/why-do-people-drink.

2. Lauren Geoffrion, "Why Alcohol Lowers Inhibitions and Leads to Bad Decisions," American Addiction Centers, updated September 5, 2023, https://alcohol.org/health-effects/inhibitions/.

3. Bob Cook, "The Next Brilliant Idea in Youth Sports Facilities: Entertaining the Parents," *Forbes*, June 26, 2018, https://www.forbes.com/sites/bobcook/2018/06/26/the-next-brilliant-idea-in-youth-sports-facilities-entertaining-the-parents/.

4. Cathy W. Hall and Raymond E. Webster, "Traumatic Symptomatology Characteristics of Adult Children of Alcoholics," *Journal of Drug Education* 32, no. 3 (September 2002): 195–211, https://doi.org/10.2190/u29w-lf3w-748l-a48m.

5. Amy Keller, "The Five Types of Alcoholics," DrugRehab.com, updated July 9, 2021, https://www.drugrehab.com/addiction/alcohol/types-of-alcoholics/.

6. National Center for Drug Abuse Statistics, "Alcohol Related Deaths per Year, State and More: 2022 Analysis," accessed May 20, 2024, https://drugabusestatistics.org/alcohol-related-deaths/.

7. Gallup, "What Percentage of Americans Drink Alcohol?" December 29, 2022, https://news.gallup.com/poll/467507/percentage-americans-drink-alcohol.aspx.

CHAPTER 9

1. Jennifer Casarella, "Signs of a Toxic Person," WebMD, December 18, 2022, https://www.webmd.com/mental-health/signs-toxic-person.

2. Elizabeth Scott, "What Is a Toxic Relationship?" Verywell Mind, updated November 3, 2023, https://www.verywellmind.com/toxic-relationships-4174665.

3. Loretta Graziano Breuning, "The Inner Mammal Institute," accessed May 21, 2024, https://innermammalinstitute.org/lorettabreuning/.

4. Mary West, "Mood Changes: Are They Mental or Hormonal?" Medical News Today, October 27, 2023, https://www.medicalnewstoday.com/articles/changes-in-mood-mental-or-hormonal#mental-causes.

5. Breuning, "Inner Mammal Institute."

6. Quoted in Scott Muska, "What Happens to Your Body and Brain When You Watch Football," Better by Today, updated February 4, 2018, https://www.nbcnews.com/better/health/what-happens-your-body-brain-when-you-watch-football-ncna814401.

7. Jason Whiting, "Is Your Fight or Flight Reflex Harming Your Relationship?" *Psychology Today*, December 28, 2022, https://www.psychologytoday.com/us/blog/love-lies-and-conflict/202212/is-your-fight-or-flight-reflex-harming-your-relationship.

8. Mental Health Foundation, "Cool Down: Anger and How to Deal with It," accessed May 21, 2024, https://www.mentalhealth.org.uk/explore-mental-health/publications/cool-down.

9. Taayoo Murray, "Does Caffeine Affect Hormones?" Checkup, February 18, 2022, https://www.singlecare.com/blog/caffeine-and-hormones.

10. Ria Health Team, "Alcohol and Hormones: Can Drinking Throw You off Balance?" Ria Health, updated August 10, 2022, https://riahealth.com/blog/alcohol-and-hormones/.

11. Eve Van Cauter, Kristen Knutson, Rachel Leproult, and Karine Spiegel, n.d. "The Impact of Sleep Deprivation on Hormones and Metabolism," Medscape, accessed May 21, 2024, https://medscape.org/viewarticle/502825.

12. Shirley Davis, "The Healing Effects on the Brain from Mindfulness, Prayer, and Meditation," CPTSD Foundation, January 30, 2020, https://cptsdfoundation.org/2020/01/30/the-healing-effects-on-the-brain-from-mindfulness-prayer-and-meditation/.

13. *Merriam-Webster.com Dictionary*, "Catalyst," accessed May 21, 2024, https://www.merriam-webster.com/dictionary/catalyst.

CHAPTER 10

1. Heather Lonczak, "What Is Positive Parenting? A Look at the Research and Benefits." PositivePsychology.com, May 8, 2019, https://positivepsychology.com/positive-parenting/.

2. Anna Schmidt, "Groupthink," *Encyclopædia Britannica*, updated May 17, 2024, https://www.britannica.com/science/groupthink.

3. Thomas Edison State University and Diana Sanchez, "The Psychology of Groups," in *An Introduction to Social Psychology* (Trenton, NJ: Thomas Edison State University, 2022), https://opened.tesu.edu/introsocialpsychology/chapter/the-psychology-of-groups/.

4. Thomas Edison State University and Sanchez, "Psychology of Groups."

5. Staff and Wire Reports, "High School Coaches Increasingly Targeted by Overbearing, Undermining Parents," TwinCities.com Pioneer Press, May 29, 2016, https://www.twincities.com/2016/05/29/high-school-coaches-increasingly-targeted-by-overbearing-undermining-parents/.

6. David La Vaque, "'Vicious Personal Attacks' Triggers Stillwater Coach Resignation," MN Girls' Hockey Hub, April 8, 2016, https://www.mngirlshockeyhub.com/news_article/show/634741.

7. Jace Frederick, "Stillwater Girls Hockey Boosters Decry 'Disgruntled Few' Who Attacked Coach," TwinCities.com Pioneer Press, updated April 14, 2016, https://www.twincities.com/2016/04/13/stillwater-girls-hockey-boosters-decry-disgruntled-few-who-attacked-coach/.

8. Courtney Blackledge, "What Is Grooming? Understanding Sexual Abuse," GoodRx Health, updated September 20, 2023, https://www.goodrx.com/health-topic/mental-health/what-is-grooming-sexual-abuse.

9. Dictionary.com, "Team," accessed May 21, 2024, https://www.dictionary.com/browse/team.

CHAPTER 11

1. Kate Greenway, interview by Larry Meiller, *The Larry Meiller Show*, Wisconsin Public Radio, October 26, 2023, https://mp3.wpr.org/download.php?f=https://wpr-podcast.streamguys1.com/mlr/mlr231026f2.mp3.

2. Bernard Golden, "How Grieving Ideas Can Be an Antidote to Chronic Anger," *Psychology Today*, June 20, 2022, https://www.psychologytoday.com/us/blog/overcoming-destructive-anger/202206/how-grieving-ideas-can-be-antidote-chronic-anger.

3. Kimberly Holland, "Stages of Grief: General Patterns for Breakups, Divorce, Loss, More," Healthline, updated May 17, 2023, https://www.healthline.com/health/stages-of-grief.

4. Psychology Today Staff, "Denial," *Psychology Today*, accessed June 4, 2024, https://www.psychologytoday.com/us/basics/denial.

5. Meagan Frank, "The Grief of Getting Cut," *Team Adult Playbook* (blog), October 6, 2012, https://theteamadultplaybook.com/2012/10/06/the-grief-of -getting-cut/.

6. Psychology Today Staff, "Anger," *Psychology Today*, accessed May 20, 2024, https://www.psychologytoday.com/us/basics/anger.

7. Golden, "Grieving Ideas."

8. Golden, "Grieving Ideas."

CHAPTER 12

1. Reinhold Niebuhr, *Moral Man and Immoral Society: A Study in Ethics and Politics* (Louisville, KY: Westminster John Knox, 2021).

2. Michael J. Hurd, "The Psychology of Status-Seeking," DrHurd.com, May 22, 2014, https://drhurd.com/2014/05/22/46112/.

3. Martin E. P. Seligman, *Authentic Happiness: Using the New Positive Psychology to Realize Your Potential for Lasting Fulfillment* (New York: Free Press, 2002).

4. Jeremy Sutton, "Martin Seligman's Positive Psychology Theory," PositivePsychology.com, October 4, 2016, https://positivepsychology.com/positive -psychology-theory/.

5. Steven C. Hayes, *A Liberated Mind: How to Pivot toward What Matters* (New York: Avery, 2019).

6. Juan Xi and Matthew T. Lee, "Inner Peace as a Contribution to Human Flourishing: A New Scale Developed from Ancient Wisdom," in *Measuring Well-Being: Interdisciplinary Perspectives from the Social Sciences and Humanities*, ed. Matthew T. Lee, Laura D. Kubzansky, and Tyler J. VanderWeele, 435–81 (New York: Oxford University Press, 2021), https://doi.org/10.1093/oso /9780197512531.003.0016.

7. Xi and Lee, "Inner Peace."

8. Tea on the Tiber, "Pema Chödrön Quotes: Embracing Life with Mindfulness and Compassion," accessed January 31, 2024, https://teaonthetiber.com/ pema-chodron-quotes/.

9. Psalms 34:15 (RSV).

10. Richard H. Schwartz, "Jewish Teachings on Peace," *Times of Israel*, October 22, 2017, https://blogs.timesofisrael.com/jewish-teachings-on-peace/.

11. 1 Cor. 13:4–8 (RSV).

12. Dawn O. Braithwaite, "Why Communication Matters," *Psychology Today*, July 15, 2021, https://www.psychologytoday.com/us/blog/communication -matters/202107/why-communication-matters.

Bibliography

Ackerman, Courtney E. "Self-Determination Theory and How It Explains Motivation." Positive Psychology. June 21, 2018. https://positivepsychology.com/self-determination-theory/.

Anderson, Cameron, and John Angus D. Hildreth. *Striving for Superiority: The Human Desire for Status*. Working Paper 115–16. Berkeley: University of California, October 2016. https://irle.berkeley.edu/wp-content/uploads/2016/10/Striving-for-superiority.pdf.

Aquinas, Thomas. *Summa of Theology I*. Q20 A1. ad. 3.

Aten, Jamie D. "What Is Joy and What Does It Say about Us?" *Psychology Today*, July 28, 2020, https://www.psychologytoday.com/us/blog/hope-resilience/202007/what-is-joy-and-what-does-it-say-about-us.

AUDIT: Alcohol Use Disorders Identification Test. "AUDIT Questionnaire." Accessed June 3, 2024. https://auditscreen.org/~auditscreen/cmsb/uploads/audit-english-version-new_001.pdf.

Balyi, Istvan, and Jim Grove. "If You're Raising a Child Athlete, Think Long-Term." Active for Life. March 11, 2013. https://activeforlife.com/raising-child-athlete-long-term/.

Balyi, Istvan, Richard Way, and Colin Higgs. *Long-Term Athlete Development*. Champaign, IL: Human Kinetics, 2013.

Barone, Emily. "The Astronomical Cost of Kids' Sports." *Time*. August 24, 2017. https://time.com/4913284/kids-sports-cost/.

Bigelow, Bob, Tom Moroney, and Linda Hall. *Just Let the Kids Play: How to Stop Other Adults from Ruining Your Child's Fun and Success in Youth Sports*. Deerfield Beach, FL: Health Communications, 2001.

Blackledge, Courtney. "What Is Grooming? Understanding Sexual Abuse." GoodRx Health. Updated September 20, 2023. https://www.goodrx.com/health-topic/mental-health/what-is-grooming-sexual-abuse.

Braithwaite, Dawn O. "Why Communication Matters." *Psychology Today*. July 15, 2021. https://www.psychologytoday.com/us/blog/communication-matters/202107/why-communication-matters.

Brandenburger, Adam M., and Barry J. Nalebuff. *Co-opetition*. New York: Doubleday, 1996.

Breuning, Loretta Graziano. The Inner Mammal Institute. Accessed May 21, 2024. https://innermammalinstitute.org/lorettabreuning/.

Brooks, Arthur C., and Oprah Winfrey. *Build the Life You Want: The Art and Science of Getting Happier*. New York: Penguin, 2023.

BVM Sportsdesk. "Minnesota Boys High School Hockey Championship Shines Brighter than NHL Games." BVM Sports. March 10, 2024. https://bvmsports.com/2024/03/10/minnesota-boys-high-school-hockey-championship-shines-brighter-than-nhl-games.

Cacciola, Scott. "There Was Always Crying in Sports. The Kelces Made It Cool." *New York Times*, March 6, 2024. https://www.nytimes.com/2024/03/06/style/jason-kelce-crying.htm.

Camera, Lauren. "More Americans Say Transgender Athletes Should Only Play for Teams That Match Gender of Birth." *U.S. News & World Report*. June 13, 2023. https://www.usnews.com/news/national-news/articles/2023-06-13/more-americans-say-transgender-athletes-should-only-play-for-teams-that-match-gender-at-birth.

Casarella, Jennifer. "Signs of a Toxic Person." WebMD. December 18, 2022. https://www.webmd.com/mental-health/signs-toxic-person.

Cashmore, Ellis. *Making Sense of Sports*. 5th ed. London: Routledge, 2010.

Cerda, Andy. "Family Time Is Far More Important than Other Aspects of Life for Most Americans." Pew Research Center. May 26, 2023. https://www.pewresearch.org/short-reads/2023/05/26/family-time-is-far-more-important-than-other-aspects-of-life-for-most-americans/.

Cherry, Kendra. "Motivation: The Driving Force behind Our Actions." Verywell Mind. Updated May 3, 2023. https://www.verywellmind.com/what-is-motivation-2795378.

Coakley, Jay J. *Sports in Society: Issues and Controversies*. 13th ed. New York: McGraw-Hill, 2021.

Coble, Cassandra, and Richard Buning. "Why Massive New Youth Sports Facilities May Not Lead to the Tourist Boom Many Communities Hope for When They Build Them." Conversation. January 18, 2022. https://theconversation.com/why-massive-new-youth-sports-facilities-may-not-lead-to-the-tourist-boom-many-communities-hope-for-when-they-build-them-173126.

Collingwood, Jane. "Teaching Your Baby Sign Language Can Benefit Both of You." PsychCentral. May 17, 2016. https://www.psychcentral.com/lib/teaching-your-baby-sign-language-can-benefit-both-of-you#1.

Cook, Bob. "The Next Brilliant Idea in Youth Sports Facilities: Entertaining the Parents." *Forbes*. June 26, 2018. https://www.forbes.com/sites/bobcook/2018/06/26/the-next-brilliant-idea-in-youth-sports-facilities-entertaining-the-parents/.

Data Commons. "Woodbury." Accessed May 21, 2024. https://datacommons.org/place/geoId/2771428.

Davis, Shirley. "The Healing Effects on the Brain from Mindfulness, Prayer, and Meditation." CPTSD Foundation. January 30, 2020. https://cptsdfoundation.org/2020/01/30/the-healing-effects-on-the-brain-from-mindfulness-prayer-and-meditation/.

Deci, Edward. *Why We Do What We Do: Understanding Self-Motivation.* New York: Penguin Books, 1995.

De Lench, Brooke C. *Home Team Advantage: The Critical Role of Mothers in Youth Sports.* New York: Collins, 2006.

Dicicco, Tony, Colleen Hacker, and Charles Salzberg. *Catch Them Being Good: Everything You Need to Know to Successfully Coach Girls.* New York: Viking, 2002.

Dictionary.com. "Team." Accessed May 21, 2024. https://www.dictionary.com/browse/team.

DiveThru Team. "Feeling Hurt: A Guide to Your Emotions." DiveThru. Updated January 26, 2023. https://divethru.com/feeling-hurt-a-guide-to-your-emotions/.

Dunkelman, Marc J. *The Vanishing Neighbor: The Transformation of American Community.* New York: W. W. Norton, 2014.

Editorial Staff, American Addiction Centers. "CAGE Questionnaire (4 Questions to Screen for Alcholism)." American Addiction Centers. Updated February 7, 2024. https://americanaddictioncenters.org/alcohol/rehab-treatment/cage-questionnaire-assessment.

Ehrmann, Joe, Paula Ehrmann, and Gregory Jordan. *InSideOut Coaching: How Sports Can Transform Lives.* New York: Simon and Schuster, 2011.

Eitzen, D. Stanley. *Fair and Foul: Beyond the Myths and Paradoxes of Sport.* Lanham, MD: Rowman & Littlefield, 2016.

Ellis, Clayton, Becky Foellmer, Mark Foellmer, Rick Howard, Robert Knipe, Ann Paulis-Neal, Lisa Paulson, and Allison Ross. *Physical Activity Should Not Be Used as Punishment and/or Behavior Management.* Annapolis Junction, MD: SHAPE America, 2021. https://www.shapeamerica.org/Common/Uploaded%20files/uploads/2021/advocacy/position-statements/Physical-Activity-Should-Not-Be-Used-as-Punishment-and-or-Behavior-Management.pdf.

Eustis, Susan. "Youth Sports Market Grows-Market Research." WinterGreen Research. Updated August 10, 2023. https://www.wintergreenresearch.com/post/youth-sports-market-grows.

Family Education. "What Boys Learn from Their Dads." Accessed May 21, 2024. https://www.familyeducation.com/family-life/dad-life/what-boys-learn-their-dads.

Farrey, Tom. *Game On: How the Pressure to Win at All Costs Endangers Youth Sports, and What Parents Can Do about It.* New York: ESPN Books, 2009.

Feinberg, Mark E., Anna R. Solmeyer, and Susan M. McHale. "The Third Rail of Family Systems: Sibling Relationships, Mental and Behavioral

Health, and Preventive Intervention in Childhood and Adolescence." *Clinical Child and Family Psychology Review* 15, no. 1 (March 2012): 43–57. https://doi.org/10.1007/s10567-011-0104-5.

Fellow, Scottie Andrew. "Five Ways High Testosterone Impacts Men's Behavior." *Newsweek*, updated July 9, 2018. https://www.newsweek.com/five-ways-high-testosterone-impacts-mens-behavior-1010705.

Firestone, Lisa. "Is Being Proud of Your Kids Really about You?" *Psychology Today*, June 14, 2017. https://www.psychologytoday.com/us/blog/compassion-matters/201706/is-being-proud-your-kids-really-about-you.

Frank, Meagan. "The Grief of Getting Cut." *Team Adult Playbook* (blog). October 6, 2012. https://theteamadultplaybook.com/2012/10/06/the-grief-of-getting-cut/.

Frederick, Jace. "Stillwater Girls Hockey Boosters Decry 'Disgruntled Few' Who Attacked Coach." TwinCities.com Pioneer Press. Updated April 14, 2016. https://www.twincities.com/2016/04/13/stillwater-girls-hockey-boosters-decry-disgruntled-few-who-attacked-coach/.

Gallup. "What Percentage of Americans Drink Alcohol?" December 29, 2022. https://news.gallup.com/poll/467507/percentage-americans-drink-alcohol.aspx.

Gauthier, Anne H., and Petra W. de Jong. "Costly Children: The Motivations for Parental Investment in Children in a Low Fertility Context." *Genus Journal of Population Sciences* 77, no. 6 (2021). https://doi.org/10.1186/s41118-020-00111-5.

Geoffrion, Lauren. "Why Alcohol Lowers Inhibitions and Leads to Bad Decisions." American Addiction Centers. Updated September 5, 2023. https://alcohol.org/health-effects/inhibitions/.

Golden, Bernard. "How Grieving Ideas Can Be an Antidote to Chronic Anger." *Psychology Today*, June 20, 2022. https://www.psychologytoday.com/us/blog/overcoming-destructive-anger/202206/how-grieving-ideas-can-be-antidote-chronic-anger.

Greenberg, Melanie. "The Neuroscience of Fairness and Injustice." *Psychology Today*, August 22, 2014. https://www.psychologytoday.com/us/blog/the-mindful-self-express/201408/the-neuroscience-fairness-and-injustice.

Gruber, June, and Jessica L. Borelli. "The Importance of Fostering Emotional Diversity in Boys." *Scientific American*, December 12, 2017. https://www.scientificamerican.com/article/the-importance-of-fostering-emotional-diversity-in-boys/.

Gurian, Michael. *Boys and Girls Learn Differently! A Guide for Teachers and Parents*. San Francisco: Jossey-Bass, 2011.

Hagan, Ekua. "What Is Joy and What Does It Say about Us?" *Psychology Today*, July 28, 2020. https://www.psychologytoday.com/us/blog/hope-resilience/202007/what-is-joy-and-what-does-it-say-about-us.

Hall, Cathy W., and Raymond E. Webster. "Traumatic Symptomatology Characteristics of Adult Children of Alcoholics." *Journal of Drug Education* 32, no. 3 (September 2002): 195–211. https://doi.org/10.2190/u29w-lf3w-748l-a48m.

Hartney, Elizabeth. "How Emotional Pain Affects Your Body." Verywell Mind. Updated May 20, 2024. https://www.verywellmind.com/physical-pain-and-emotional-pain-22421.

Hayes, Steven C. *A Liberated Mind: How to Pivot toward What Matters.* New York: Avery, 2019.

Heshmat, Shahram. "Why Do People Drink?" *Psychology Today,* March 3, 2017. https://www.psychologytoday.com/us/blog/science-choice/201703/why-do-people-drink.

Higbee, Eric. "Why the Three Rings of Community Are So Important." The Answer Is Community. March 7, 2023. https://www.theanswseris.community/the-three-rings-of-community-and-why-they-are-so-important.

Higgs, Colin, Richard Way, Vicki Harber, Paul Jurbala, and Istvan Balyi. *Long-Term Development in Sport and Physical Activity 3.0.* Victoria, BC: Sport for Life, 2019. https://sportforlife.ca/wp-content/uploads/2019/06/Long-Term-Development-in-Sport-and-Physical-Activity-3.0.pdf.

Hobson, Will. "The Fight for the Future of Transgender Athletes." *Washington Post,* April 15, 2021. https://www.washingtonpost.com/sports/2021/04/15/transgender-athletes-womens-sports-title-ix/.

Holland, Kimberly. "Stages of Grief: General Patterns for Breakups, Divorce, Loss, More." Healthline. Updated May 17, 2023. https://www.healthline.com/health/stages-of-grief.

Hoyt, Alia. "How Crying Works." HowStuffWorks. Updated June 9, 2023. https://science.howstuffworks.com/life/inside-the-mind/emotions/crying.htm.

Hurd, Michael J. "The Psychology of Status-Seeking." DrHurd.com. May 22, 2014. https://drhurd.com/2014/05/22/46112/.

Hyman, Mark. *The Most Expensive Game in Town: The Rising Cost of Youth Sports and the Toll on Today's Families.* Boston: Beacon Press, 2013.

Iannelli, Vincent. "When Should Puberty Start in Girls and Boys?" Verywell Family. Updated April 5, 2022. https://www.verywellfamily.com/when-should-puberty-start-2632063.

Jäncke, Lutz. "Sex/Gender Differences in Cognition, Neurophysiology, and Neuroanatomy." *F1000Research* 7 (June 20, 2018): 805. https://doi.org/10.12688/f1000research.13917.1.

Johns Hopkins Medicine. "The Benefits of Playing with Your Child." Accessed May 21, 2024. https://www.hopkinsmedicine.org/health/wellness-and-prevention/the-benefits-of-playing-with-your-child.

Keller, Amy. "The Five Types of Alcoholics." DrugRehab.com. Updated July 9, 2021. https://www.drugrehab.com/addiction/alcohol/types-of-alcoholics/.

Koller, Dionne, and Han Xiao. *Passing the Torch: Modernizing Olympic, Paralympic, and Grassroots Sports in America*. N.p.: Commission on the State of U.S. Olympics & Paralympics, 2024. https://www.csusop.org/.

Koss, Maddie. "No, They're Not Boys. But Madison Soccer Team Endures Criticism Because Players Have Short Hair." *Milwaukee Journal Sentinel*, August 5, 2017. https://www.jsonline.com/story/news/2017/08/05/madison-girls-soccer-team-bristles-critics-who-say-players-boys/459741001/.

La Vaque, David. "'Vicious Personal Attacks' Triggers Stillwater Coach Resignation." MN Girls' Hockey Hub. April 8, 2016. https://www.mngirlshockeyhub.com/news_article/show/634741.

Lehman, James. "How to Give Kids Consequences That Work." EmpoweringParents.com. Accessed May 21, 2024. https://www.empoweringparents.com/article/how-to-give-kids-consequences-that-work/.

LoBue, Vanessa. "What Our Faces Say to Our Children." *Psychology Today*, September 14, 2020. https://www.psychologytoday.com/us/blog/the-baby-scientist/202009/what-our-faces-say-our-children.

Lonczak, Heather. "What Is Positive Parenting? A Look at the Research and Benefits." PositivePsychology.com. May 8, 2019. https://positivepsychology.com/positive-parenting/.

Lynch, Jerry. *Let Them Play: The Power and Joy of Mindful Sports Parenting*. Novato, CA: New World Library, 2016.

Marshall, Penny, dir. *A League of Their Own*. Culver City, CA: Columbia Pictures, 1993.

Massachusetts General Hospital and Harvard Medical School. "Harvard Second Generation Study." Accessed June 13, 2024. https://www.adultdevelopmentstudy.org/.

Matthias, Dawn R. Letter to Joe Zydowsky, September 11, 2019. United States Department of Education Office for Civil Rights. https://www2.ed.gov/about/offices/list/ocr/docs/investigations/more/05171450-a.pdf.

McCarthy, Paul J., Marc V. Jones, and David Clark-Carter. "Understanding Enjoyment in Youth Sport: A Developmental Perspective." *Psychology of Sport and Exercise* 9, no. 2 (March 2008): 142–56. https://doi.org/10.1016/j.psychsport.2007.01.005.

Mcleod, Saul. "Maslow's Hierarchy of Needs." Simply Psychology. Updated January 24, 2024. https://www.simplypsychology.org/maslow.html.

Meiller, Larry. Interview with Kate Greenway. *The Larry Meiller Show*. Wisconsin Public Radio. October 26, 2023. https://mp3.wpr.org/download.php?f=https://wpr-podcast.streamguys1.com/mlr/mlr231026f2.mp3.

Mental Health Foundation. "Cool Down: Anger and How to Deal with It." Accessed May 21, 2024. https://www.mentalhealth.org.uk/explore-mental-health/publications/cool-down.

Merriam-Webster.com Dictionary. "Catalyst." Accessed May 21, 2024. https://www.merriam-webster.com/dictionary/catalyst.

———. "Pride." Accessed May 21, 2024. https://www.merriam-webster.com/dictionary/pride.

Milken Institute School of Public Health. "Amanda J. Visek." George Washington University. Accessed May 21, 2024. https://publichealth.gwu.edu/departments/exercise-and-nutrition-sciences/amanda-visek.

Minnesota Hockey. "Minnesota Hockey Replaces Residency Rule with Participation Rule." Rogers Youth Hockey Association. October 3, 2009. https://www.rogershockey.com/news_article/show/31348.

Mountjoy, Margo, Jorunn Sundgot-Borgen, Louise Burke, Susan Carter, Naama Constantini, Constance Lebrun, Nanna Meyer, et al. "The IOC Consensus Statement: Beyond the Female Athlete Triad—Relative Energy Deficiency in Sport (RED-S)." *British Journal of Sports Medicine* 48, no. 7 (April 2014). https://doi.org/10.1136/bjsports-2014-093502.

Murray, Taayoo. "Does Caffeine Affect Hormones?" Checkup. February 18, 2022. https://www.singlecare.com/blog/caffeine-and-hormones.

Muska, Scott. "What Happens to Your Body and Brain When You Watch Football." Better by Today. Updated February 4, 2018. https://www.nbcnews.com/better/health/what-happens-your-body-brain-when-you-watch-football-ncna814401.

National Center for Drug Abuse Statistics. "Alcohol Related Deaths per Year, State and More: 2022 Analysis." Accessed May 20, 2024. https://drugabusestatistics.org/alcohol-related-deaths/.

Nelson, Mariah Burton. *The Stronger Women Get, the More Men Love Football: Sexism and the American Culture of Sports.* New York: Harcourt Brace, 1994.

New York Lawyers for the Public Interest. "Court Approves Landmark Sports Equity Class Action Settlement, Increasing Access to Sports for Black and Latinx High School Students." Press release. March 10, 2022. https://www.nylpi.org/court-approves-landmark-sports-equity-class-action-settlement-increasing-access-to-sports-for-black-and-latinx-high-school-students/.

Niebuhr, Reinhold. *Moral Man and Immoral Society: A Study in Ethics and Politics.* Louisville, KY: Westminster John Knox, 2021.

Ocklenburg, Sebastian. "13 Surprising Scientific Findings about Crying." *Psychology Today*, September 17, 2020. https://www.psychologytoday.com/us/blog/the-asymmetric-brain/202009/13-surprising-scientific-findings-about-crying.

O'Hara, Delia. "The Intrinsic Motivation of Richard Ryan and Edward Deci." American Psychological Association. 2017. https://www.apa.org/members/content/intrinsic-motivation.

O'Sullivan, John. *Changing the Game: The Parent's Guide to Raising Happy, High Performing Athletes, and Giving Youth Sports Back to Our Kids.* New York: Morgan James, 2013.

Oxford Learner's Dictionaries. "Pride." Accessed May 21, 2024. https://www.oxfordlearnersdictionaries.com/definition/english/pride_1.

Project Play. "Children's Bill of Rights in Sports." Aspen Institute. Accessed May 21, 2024. https://projectplay.org/childrens-rights-and-sports.

———. "Physical and Mental Health Trends." Aspen Institute. Accessed May 21, 2024. https://projectplay.org/state-of-play-2022/physical-mental-health-trends.

———. "Youth Sports Facts: Challenges." Aspen Institute. Accessed May 21, 2024. https://projectplay.org/youth-sports-facts/challenges.

Psychology Today Staff. "Anger." *Psychology Today.* Accessed May 20, 2024. https://www.psychologytoday.com/us/basics/anger.

———. "Denial." *Psychology Today.* Accessed June 4, 2024. https://www.psychologytoday.com/us/basics/denial.

The Recovery Village Drug and Alcohol Rehab. "MAST Alcohol Assessment: The Michigan Alcohol Screening Test (Free)." Accessed June 3, 2024. https://www.therecoveryvillage.com/alcohol-abuse/mast-alcohol-assessment-quiz/.

Research and Markets. "Youth Sports Market Projected to Reach $77.6 Billion by 2026—Comprehensive Industry Analysis and Insights." GlobeNewswire. December 26, 2019. https://www.globenewswire.com/news-release/2019/12/26/1964575/0/en/Youth-Sports-Market-Projected-to-Reach-77-6-Billion-by-2026-Comprehensive-Industry-Analysis-Insights.html.

Resolution Agreement, Menomonie Area School District. Office of Civil Rights case no. 05-17-1450. Accessed May 21, 2024. https://www2.ed.gov/about/offices/list/ocr/docs/investigations/more/05171450-b.pdf.

Ria Health Team. "Alcohol and Hormones: Can Drinking Throw You off Balance?" Ria Health. Updated August 10, 2022. https://riahealth.com/blog/alcohol-and-hormones/.

Roan, Dan, and Katie Falkingham. "Transgender Athletes: What Do the Scientists Say?" BBC Sport. May 11, 2022. https://www.bbc.com/sport/61346517.

Rosalind Franklin University. "Massive Study Reveals Few Differences between Men and Women's Brains." Neuroscience News. March 25, 2021. https://neurosciencenews.com/brain-sex-differences-18107/.

Ryan, Richard M., and Edward L. Deci. "Self-Determination Theory and the Facilitation of Intrinsic Motivation, Social Development, and Well-Being." *American Psychologist* 55, no. 1 (January 2000): 68–78. https://doi.org/10.1037//0003-066x.55.1.68.

Schmidt, Anna. "Groupthink." *Encyclopædia Britannica.* Updated May 17, 2024. https://www.britannica.com/science/groupthink.

Schwartz, Richard H. "Jewish Teachings on Peace." *Times of Israel,* October 22, 2017. https://blogs.timesofisrael.com/jewish-teachings-on-peace/.

Scott, Elizabeth. "What Is a Toxic Relationship?" Verywell Mind. Updated November 3, 2023. https://www.verywellmind.com/toxic-relationships-4174665.

Seligman, Martin E. P. *Authentic Happiness: Using the New Positive Psychology to Realize Your Potential for Lasting Fulfillment.* New York: Free Press, 2002.

Sheffield, Bryon. "2023 Annual Soccer Parent Survey Report!" Soccer Parenting. January 22, 2024. https://www.soccerparenting.com/2023-annual-soccer-parent-survey-report/.

Simmons, Rachel. *Odd Girl Out: The Hidden Culture of Aggression in Girls.* New York: Mariner Books, 2011.

Sinha, Rajita. "Alcohol's Negative Emotional Side: The Role of Stress Neurobiology in Alcohol Use Disorder." *Alcohol Research: Current Reviews* 42, no. 1 (October 27, 2022). https://arcr.niaaa.nih.gov/volume/42/1/alcohols-negative-emotional-side-role-stress-neurobiology-alcohol-use-disorder.

Staff and Wire Reports. "High School Coaches Increasingly Targeted by Overbearing, Undermining Parents." TwinCities.com Pioneer Press. May 29, 2016. https://www.twincities.com/2016/05/29/high-school-coaches-increasingly-targeted-by-overbearing-undermining-parents/.

Stanborough, Rebecca Joy. "Concrete Thinking: Building Block, Stumbling Block, or Both?" Healthline. August 30, 2019. https://www.healthline.com/health/concrete-thinking.

Storr, Will. *The Status Game.* London: William Collins, 2021.

St-Pierre, Marilou. "The Inclusion of Trans and Non-Binary People in Sport: It's a Matter for Everyone!" Sport for Life webinar, January 25, 2024.

Sutton, Jeremy. "Martin Seligman's Positive Psychology Theory." Positive-Psychology.com. October 4, 2016. https://positivepsychology.com/positive-psychology-theory/.

Taylor, Jim. "Develop Emotional Mastery in Your Young Athletes." *Psychology Today*, October 16, 2017. https://www.psychologytoday.com/us/blog/the-power-prime/201710/develop-emotional-mastery-in-your-young-athletes.

———. *Raising Young Athletes: Parenting Your Children to Victory in Sports and Life.* Lanham, MD: Rowman & Littlefield, 2018.

Taylor, Shelley E. "Tend and Befriend: Biobehavioral Bases of Affiliation under Stress." *Current Directions in Psychological Science* 15, no. 6 (December 2006): 273–77. https://www.jstor.org/stable/20183134.

Tea on the Tiber. "Pema Chödrön Quotes: Embracing Life with Mindfulness and Compassion." Accessed January 31, 2024. https://teaonthetiber.com/pema-chodron-quotes/.

Thomas Edison State University and Diana Sanchez. "The Psychology of Groups." In *An Introduction to Social Psychology.* Trenton, NJ: Thomas Edison State University, 2022. https://opened.tesu.edu/introsocialpsychology/chapter/the-psychology-of-groups/.

Thompson, Derek. "American Meritocracy Is Killing Youth Sports." *Atlantic*, November 6, 2018. https://www.theatlantic.com/ideas/archive/2018/11/income-inequality-explains-decline-youth-sports/574975/.

Thompson, Jim. *Positive Sports Parenting: How "Second-Goal" Parents Raise Winners in Life through Sports*. Portola Valley, CA: Balance Sports, 2008.

Tracy, Jessica. *Pride: The Secret of Success*. New York: HarperOne, 2016.

Tracy, Jessica L. "Pride: It Brings Out the Best—and Worst—in Humans." *Scientific American*, November 1, 2013. https://www.scientificamerican.com/article/pride-it-brings-out-the-best-and-worst-in-humans/.

United Nations Department of Economic and Social Affairs. "Addressing Climate Change through Sport." Policy Brief 128. January 2022. https://www.un.org/development/desa/dpad/wp-content/uploads/sites/45/PB_128.pdf.

Vaillant, George. "Your Childhood Is Crucial to How You'll Age." Next Avenue. October 31, 2013. https://www.nextavenue.org/why-your-childhood-crucial-how-youll-age/.

Van Cauter, Eve, Kristen Knutson, Rachel Leproult, and Karine Spiegel. "The Impact of Sleep Deprivation on Hormones and Metabolism." Medscape. Accessed May 21, 2024. https://medscape.org/viewarticle/502825.

Visek, Amanda J., Heather Mannix, Avinash Chandran, Sean D. Cleary, Karen A. McDonnell, and Loretta DiPietro. "Toward Understanding Youth Athletes' Fun Priorities: An Investigation of Sex, Age, and Levels of Play." *Women in Sport and Physical Activity Journal* 28, no. 1 (April 2020): 34–49. https://doi.org/10.1123/wspaj.2018-0004.

Weinberg, Robert S., and Daniel Gould. *Foundations of Sport and Exercise Psychology*. 5th ed. Champaign, IL: Human Kinetics, 2011.

West, Mary. "Mood Changes: Are They Mental or Hormonal?" Medical News Today. October 27, 2023. https://www.medicalnewstoday.com/articles/changes-in-mood-mental-or-hormonal#mental-causes.

Whiting, Jason. "Is Your Fight or Flight Reflex Harming Your Relationship?" *Psychology Today*, December 28, 2022. https://www.psychologytoday.com/us/blog/love-lies-and-conflict/202212/is-your-fight-or-flight-reflex-harming-your-relationship.

Wilson, John. "That's Why They Call It Play: The Joy of Sports." Filmed May 15, 2014, in Charleston, SC. TED video, 10:17. https://youtu.be/ra7uJtVj1bI?si=LxNS5VGkCUDTYCgj.

Wilson, Lindsey. "The Lifelong Pursuit of Joy in Sports." *Positive Performance Training* (blog). June 1, 2022. https://www.positiveperformancetraining.com/blog/the-lifelong-pursuit-of-cultivating-joy-in-sports.

Wiseman, Rosalind. *Queen Bees and Wannabes: Helping Your Daughter Survive Cliques, Gossip, Boys, and the New Realities of Girl World*. 3rd ed. New York: Harmony Books, 2016.

Xi, Juan, and Matthew T. Lee. "Inner Peace as a Contribution to Human Flourishing: A New Scale Developed from Ancient Wisdom." In *Measuring Well-Being: Interdisciplinary Perspectives from the Social Sciences and Humanities*, edited by Matthew T. Lee, Laura D. Kubzansky, and Tyler J. VanderWeele, 435–81. New York: Oxford University Press, 2021. https://doi.org/10.1093/oso/9780197512531.003.0016.

Zeigler, Mark. "Column: Norway's Hands-Off Approach to Youth Sports Might Explain Why They're So Good When They Get Older." *San Diego Union-Tribune*, July 20, 2022. https://www.sandiegouniontribune.com/sports/sports-columnists/story/2022-07-20/zeigler-norway-youth-sports-track-field-world-athletics-championships-eugene-karsten-warholm.

INDEX

About the Author

Meagan Frank has been a part of nearly two hundred sports communities since her time as an athlete at Colorado College, where she played NCAA Division I soccer and Division III basketball. She has experience as a coach for boys' and girls' teams at the college, high school, and youth levels; has parented three active athletes; and has held board positions for four sports associations. She is married to a coach who has coached college- and high-school-aged hockey players for more than twenty years. She has been writing since she was seven and has been drawn mostly to research journalism for more than a decade.

www.ingramcontent.com/pod-product-compliance
Lightning Source LLC
Chambersburg PA
CBHW070824100426
42813CB00003B/482